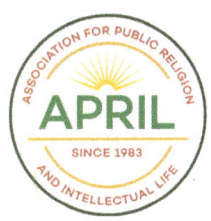

CROSSCURRENTS
PURSUING SOCIAL JUSTICE AND INTERRELIGIOUS WORK
SINCE 1950

CrossCurrents (ISSN 0011-1953; online ISSN 1939-3881) connects the wisdom of the heart with the life of the mind and the experiences of the body. The journal is operated through its parent organization, the Association for Public Religion and Intellectual Life (APRIL), an interreligious network of academics, activists, artists, and community leaders seeking to engage the many ways religion meets the public. Contributions to the journal exist at the nexus of religion, education, the arts, and social justice. The journal is published quarterly on behalf of the Association for Public Religion and Intellectual Life by the University of North Carolina Press.

The Association for Public Religion and Intellectual Life (formerly ARIL) is a global network of leaders, scholars, and social change agents who explore religious life, engage in intellectual inquiry, and lead ethical action in the world today. Their primary objective, especially through annual summer colloquia and *CrossCurrents*, is to bring together leading voices of our time to advocate for justice and to examine global spiritual and interreligious currents in both historical and contemporary perspectives.

A membership to APRIL includes access to *CrossCurrents* starting with Volume 58, 2008, though our partners at Project MUSE, monthly newsletters, early access to summer colloquium themes, a 40% on UNC Press books, and more. For more information, including membership and subscription rates, visit www.aprilonline.org.

This reissue of *CrossCurrents* was one of four issues published in 2015 as part of Volume 65. For a current masthead visit www.aprilonline.org.

© 2015 Association for Public Religion and Intellectual Life. All rights reserved.

ISBN 978-1-4696-6690-7 (Print)

CROSSCURRENTS

ANTI-SEMITISM AND ISLAMOPHOBIA: PROBING THE HISTORY AND DYNAMICS OF HATE

292
Introduction:
Anti-Semitism and Islamophobia: Twins or Category Mistake?
Björn Krondorfer

297
Sticks and Stones: The Role of Law in the Dynamics of Hate
David Kader

302
Renewed Hate:
The Place of Jews and Muslims in Contemporary White Power Thought
C. Richard King

311
Making Enemies: The Uses and Abuses of Tainted Identities
Alex Alvarez

321
Islamophobia and Anti-Semitism: Shared Prejudice or Singular Social Pathologies
Michael Dobkowski

334
Classifying Muslims
Mohamed Mosaad Abdelaziz Mohamed

346
Nostalgia and Memory in Jewish–Muslim Encounters
Mehnaz M. Afridi

357
Shifting Hierarchies of Exclusion:
Colonialism, Anti-Semitism, and Islamophobia in European History
Ethan B. Katz

371
Outlawing the Veil, Banning the Muslim?
Restricting Religious Freedom in France
Melanie Adrian

380
When the Victims are not so Innocent:
Extremist Muslim Activity in Western Bloc Countries
Khaleel Mohammed

392
The Nexus of Enmity:
Ideology, Global Politics, and Identity in the Twenty-First Century
Eyal Bar

401
Notes on Contributors

CROSSCURRENTS

INTRODUCTION: ANTI-SEMITISM AND ISLAMOPHOBIA
Twins or Category Mistake?

Björn Krondorfer

As guest editor of this *CrossCurrents* issue, I would like to address a question that I have been asked frequently: Why do you mention anti-Semitism and Islamophobia in one breath? What is the use and value of investigating them together?

By mentioning them side by side, do we suggest similarity, parallelism, or analogy? Or, to the contrary, do we compare them in order to highlight significant differences between the two? And if we were to point out differences, do we do so because we want to gain analytical precision in terms of historical origins and social causes, or because we want to establish a hierarchy of gravity that defines one form of discrimination as being more severe than the other?

Just as Muslims and Jews, according to the religious traditions, are brothers of the same father Abraham, we might be tempted to see Muslims and Jews conjoined by the hatreds directed against them. In this case, we would look at anti-Semitism and Islamophobia as twin phenomena. It is, however, also possible that the supposed Abrahamic kinship compels us to erroneously pull two things together that should be kept apart. In this case, we might be guilty of committing a category mistake because we are presuming too strong a family resemblance between anti-Semitism and Islamophobia that renders our analysis fraudulent.

If we were to take apart the compound words "anti-Semitism" and "Islamo-phobia," we might need to conclude that a comparison constitutes, indeed, a category mistake since each term seems to point to an altogether different nature. Whereas anti-Semitism suggests opposition to "Semitism," Islamophobia suggests an irrational fear (phobia) of a religion. The latter, hence, singles out Islam as the trigger of fear, whereas anti-Semitism does not specify the source or target of its opposition. As a matter of fact, anti-Semitism could theoretically indicate opposition to Jews *and* Muslims, since both people have been classified as "Semites."

A better parallelism, therefore, might be to pair Islamophobia with Judeophobia, or anti-Judaism with anti-Muslimism, or anti-Semitism with anti-Islamism. Others have suggested that a better solution would be to speak of anti-Muslim racism, which would parallel an understanding of anti-Semitism as a form of anti-Jewish racism.

This ambiguity of terminology gets compounded by the fact that the sources and causes of ideological hatreds, irrational fears, and discriminatory practices cannot easily be determined: Are they primarily religious in nature? Are they the result of economic and social inequities? Are they the result of politically convenient mechanisms of scapegoating? Are they products of modernity (nineteenth century racist theories, colonialism, nation-building, etc)? Or, to the contrary, do they constitute enduring historical hostilities going back to the third century *Adversus Judaeos* traditions (when Christian writers began polemicizing against Jews) and to the eleventh century Christian crusades against Muslims in the Holy Land? Are they the result of political manipulations, or do they articulate a moral panic? Are anti-Semitism and Islamophobia altogether imaginary, or are they grounded in some kind of historical and contemporary experience?

The situation gets further complicated by the fact that in current popular discourse and public debates, both anti-Semitism and Islamophobia are used to score political points. To name just one example: In trying to comprehend the recent rise of anti-Semitism in Europe and other countries, scholars and the public alike have often labeled it "new anti-Semitism." This label is used to explain the recurrence of ancient stereotypes and the contemporary anti-Jewish attitudes by Muslim immigrant populations and radical political groups. At times, fingers are pointed directly at Arabs and Muslims in general; or the Qur'an is singled out among sacred scriptures as the source for Jew-hatred. Conversely, we find comments that speak of "Islamophobia as the new anti-Semitism," a usage that clearly suggests that the old hatreds directed at Jews (especially in Europe) have been replaced by the (new) hatred against Muslims. Needless to say, in either case Muslim and Jewish communities are pitted against each other. Rather than sharing a common experience of facing fears and hatreds directed at Muslims and Jews, the experience of anti-Semitism and Islamophobia deepens the mistrust between these two communities.

If the extensive scholarship on anti-Semitism and Islamophobia is any indication, we are far from gaining consensus on these complex and complicated issues. It might very well be that terminological, definitional, and theoretical clarity—as desirable as that would be—cannot be achieved. Such persistent ambiguity, however, does not change the social reality of irrational fears, ideological hatreds, and discriminatory practices that real people and communities experience and that also guide (or misguide) domestic social policies and international politics. Real people—Muslims and Jews—experience social exclusion and discrimination in their respective environments: They are heedlessly or willfully misperceived by others; they are questioned about their (national and cultural) loyalties in their countries of residence; they are turned into objects of fear; they are ridiculed for their cultural customs and religious beliefs; or they are subjected to verbal abuse; and, in the worst case, to violent and sometimes lethal assaults.

I contend that the terms "anti-Semitism" and "Islamophobia"—imperfect as they might be—are valuable insofar as they capture the breadth and depths of a variety of discriminatory and exclusionary practices without narrowing them down to a singular cause, origin, or explanation. If by anti-Semitism we mean the dread, hatred, and hostility toward Jews and Judaism, and by Islamophobia we refer to the dread, hatred, and hostility toward Muslims and Islam, we have gained a flexible working definition. It may lack analytical precision but it does allow us to enter into an informed and open-minded conversation, largely free of polemics and parochial partiality.

Each term has, of course, its own history. "Anti-Semitism" was coined in 1881 by the German publicist Wilhelm Marr. Predating the Holocaust by more than fifty years, it was exclusively reserved for Jews. Marr's intention was to find a term that would explain more persuasively the need to exclude Jews from European secular society than the older religiously based Jew-hatred still popular at the time. Marr considered religious prejudices outdated and "unscientific." Anti-Semitism, hence, came to describe the Jews as a "race." This change signaled exclusion on racial grounds, which eventually morphed into the lethal idea of Jews as a *Fremdkörper* (foreign body) that would pollute the purity of the nation-state. "Islamophobia" was first used in 1922 by the French scholar Étienne Dinet, but fell into disregard until the 1990s. Generally speaking, it is a term that indicates, as in the case of Wilhelm Marr, a dislike of Islam and Muslims from a secular Western perspective.

What makes both terms so powerful and persuasive is that they do not single out any specific cause or target. Its force lies precisely in its ambiguity: One moment the target is the religion itself (Islam is violent, literalist, backward; Judaism is anti-modern, exclusivist, legalistic), while at the next moment the focus is on individuals to whom all kinds of negative characteristics are attributed. The target may also be Jewish and Muslim culture (food, family law, lack of civility), or it may focus on collective identity through political representation (Islamic despotism, ISIS, Israel, AIPAC, etc). In most cases, however, Muslims and Jews are portrayed, criticized, ridiculed, or condemned not as real people but as fictive figures. Instances and patterns are searched and found that confirm images of "the Jew" or "the Muslim." These fictions are (re)created in endless repetitions with small variations.

In this issue on "Anti-Semitism and Islamophobia: Probing the History and Dynamics of Hate," we regard the terms Islamophobia and anti-Semitism helpful in two ways:

First, they encompass a wide spectrum of discursive practices in which prejudicial fictive images and exclusionary social mechanisms are formed, confirmed, and maintained. They cannot be reduced to culture alone, or religion alone, or political manipulations alone, or racial/racist characterizations alone, etc.

Second, they allow us to analyze these two phenomena from a similarly wide spectrum of scholarship in which different disciplinary perspectives enrich and enhance each other. Anti-Semitism and Islamophobia cannot be explained by religious studies alone, or individually by any other discipline such as political science, social psychology, law, history, etc.

Despite the existing extensive scholarly and popular literature on anti-Semitism and Islamophobia, in most cases these publications focus on either Islamophobia or anti-Semitism separately and individually. They rarely engage each other in conversation. This division of scholarly labor—whether intentional or not—often encourages claims regarding degrees of severity that are unique to either Jewish or Muslims communities. Such claims easily become competitive, therefore (inadvertently) pitting the communities against each other.

The contributions to this volume are trying to avoid this trap. Many of the articles gathered here grew out of a scholarly symposium held in October 2014 at Northern Arizona University. The symposium was called, "Muslims and Jews: Challenging the Dynamics of Hate." It was co-organized by the Martin-Springer Institute of Northern Arizona University and the United States Holocaust Memorial Museum's Mandel Center for Advanced Holocaust Studies. The contributions to this *CrossCurrents* issue are published independently from the 2014 symposium; they reflect the views of the individual authors but not the views of the USHMM or the Martin-Springer Institute.

The dialogical spirit with which the symposium was conducted is, we hope, also discernible in this journal. As contributing scholars, we are aiming at opening new venues of conversation across disciplinary perspectives rather than entrenching positions that render impossible a comparative analysis of anti-Semitism and Islamophobia. We hope that the reader will find these contributions informative and thought-provoking, and that they help to dispel misconceptions and mistrust.

CROSSCURRENTS

STICKS AND STONES
The Role of Law in the Dynamics of Hate

David Kader

>Sticks and stones will break my bones
>But words will never harm me.

So goes the famous English language children's rhyme of uncertain origins; though apparently first appears in print in the second half of the nineteenth century, with variations (for example, "Sticks and stones *may* break my bones, but words will never *hurt* me"). In either formulation, the teaching is clear, namely that children are to develop the proverbial "thick skin" to insults, taunts, and, if you will, to "turn the other cheek." The rhyme is not descriptive, but prescriptive. It is aspirational. This attitude, in my view, is not the cause of but the expression of something unique to the American story in both our culture and our law: That expression is to be tolerated no matter how vile, and that certainly there ought to be no physical retaliation by the individual. That posture of toleration is to be seen not just in the subject of the words, but in the community at large through civic action—in laws, for example. We know, however, that words do harm and can hurt—and that is not only (though especially so) to those subject to hateful words, but also to those that hurl such language at another. Both victim and victimizer recognize that words do harm, do hurt. Moreover, we also know that words can lead to action, in the speaker, in others. Hateful speech can produce hateful conduct. In short, the dynamics of hate is intimately involved with ideas and the expression of those ideas. In my contribution, then, I wish to sketch how the law relates to such dynamics, primarily in the United States, but with passing reference to comparative national and international developments elsewhere in the world.

Laws on hate speech

First a word about "sticks and stones" that may or do break bones. Such violence is, of course, subject to the criminal law and civil liability. Absent excuse or justification, causing physical harm to another is a crime and a tort. Of interest here is whether such conduct, if motivated by hate, ought to receive additional sanction, beyond the underlying wrongful behavior. The label commonly affixed to such behavior is hate crime—bias-motivated criminal behavior. The bias can be related to any number of identities: from nationality and ethnicity to religion or sexual orientation. Where legislation exists that defines hate crimes, typically by imposing greater penalties for bias-motivated conduct, they are to be understood as distinct from laws that might prohibit hate speech. What joins the debate between hate crimes and hate speech is they were both largely born out of World War II and the Holocaust. Numerous nations throughout Europe have hate crimes legislation, something that has come very slowly and piecemeal to the United States (given our federal system where criminal legislation is largely a matter of state law). Some such crimes, though, date from just after the Civil War, with the major federal legislation in this area adopted as part of the famous Civil Rights Act of 1968. Most states in the union now have some form of hate crime legislation.

While there remains some debate over the appropriateness and even efficacy of hate crime legislation, the major debate—we might even call it a controversy—is related to hate speech prohibition or regulation. If it is true that hateful speech can hurt and harm an individual, despite the admonition in the children's rhyme that it will not or ought not, and that such expression can be the foundational element in the dynamic of hate that leads to acts of violence, ought it be the subject of the law as well?

Even a cursory review of the legal landscape on this question in the United States and around the world reveals a remarkably distinct pattern. The United States has resisted prohibiting or seriously regulating hate speech, while other nations—mostly in Europe, but also elsewhere—to various degrees have legislation regarding hate speech. The same is true as to international law. The subject is vast and beyond the scope of these brief remarks—but I wish to alert those interested to a number of excellent treatments of the subject. The anthologies *The Content and Context of Hate Speech: Rethinking Regulation and Response* (Herz and Molnar 2012) and *Extreme Speech and Democracy* (Hare and Weinstein 2009) both survey the United States and other national legal developments as well as critically evaluate the merits and demerits of the myriad of approaches taken. I also highly recommend Jeremy Waldron's *The Harm in Hate Speech* (2012), which offers a thorough defense of hate speech regulation, which is a contrarian view in the American context. Obviously, there is a vast scholarly treatment of this topic, but I very much wish to share these titles. With that said, I now wish to sketch the legal landscape regarding hate speech, drawing greatly on the scholarship I have cited.

In the United States, given our First Amendment to the U.S. Constitution and its interpretation by the U.S. Supreme Court, prohibition or regulation of speech, by either the federal or state governments, is only constitutional if the speech falls into certain categories that are deemed not protected by the First Amendment. They include the following:

1 Fighting words (Chaplinsky v. N.H., 315 U.S. 568 [1942]).
2 Obscenity (Roth v. U.S., 354 U.S. 476 [1957]).
3 Defamation (N.Y. Times v. Sullivan, 376 U.S. 254 [1964]).
4 Direct incitement (Brandenburg v. Ohio, 395 U.S. 444 [1969]).
5 Immediate threats of intimidation (Virginia v. Black, 538 U.S. 343 [2003]).

Thus, where speech, including hate speech, might fall within these categories, it can be proscribed. However, no prohibition is permitted of such speech—hateful though it might be—merely due to its content. In short, there is very broad protection to speech in this country that, I think, is captured succinctly by Justice Holmes when he stated in a 1929 opinion: "If there is any principle of the Constitution that more imperatively calls for attachment than any other it is the principle of free thought—not free thought for those who agree with us but freedom for thought that we hate" (dissenting in U.S. v. Schwimmer, 279 U.S. 644, 654–55).

A cursory review of hate speech jurisprudence around the world reveals that decisions in Australia, Canada, and the continent of Europe (especially in Germany and France, as prime examples, and the United Kingdom as well) all regulate to varying degrees hate speech. Germany might be seen as one of the strongest regulators of hate speech, no doubt, due to the recognition that Nazi propaganda (speech) was instrumental in leading to the Holocaust. Germany, for example, criminalizes Holocaust denial.

International law, through UN covenants and tribunals—particularly those overseeing atrocities in Rwanda and the former Yugoslavia—likewise are prepared to punish hate speech.

What can account for this variation, particularly the resistance in the U.S. to permitting the regulation of hate speech, is undoubtedly a complex matter. But permit me to cite the views expressed by Stephen Holmes in his essay "Waldron, Machiavelli, and Hate speech":

> The answer lies in different historical experiences. On the European side, Nazism is the main issue. Here in the United States, liberals experienced the loyalty programs, commie hunting, McCarthy, the Smith Act, among other things. ….Sociology might be much more important than reason. …The difference between Americans on the one hand…and Europeans on the other lies in the relative intensity of the fear of regulation and the fear of behavior to be regulated. (Holmes 2012, 346–347)

We know, we understand the consequence of the use of sticks and stones on our bones; and I believe we appreciate the hurt/harm that words can inflict on individuals and ultimately on society. In turn, we prohibit the former, but here in this nation that celebrates liberty we refuse to regulate the latter. If that remains the status quo, and maybe it should, we need words of consolation, of empathy, of tolerance and truth to exceed or at least match words of hate. We need an ethics of speech as much if not more than the law on hate speech. I offer a few reflections on such an ethic out of my own religious tradition.

Lashon hara

Speech that says something negative about another is forbidden, even if it is true (unless the information is needed by another, like "need to know" or references). This is all the more true, then, for hateful speech. In Hebrew, such speech is known as *lashon hara* (literally, evil tongue). This term is used comprehensively, capturing a wide range of hurtful talk: from slanderous gossip to insulting disparagements, from lies to mockery. Forbidding such speech is demanded because of the intimate relationship between speech and conduct. Indeed, Jewish tradition likens gossip and murder, both metaphorically and literally! One can crush the soul of the person; one's hateful and hurtful speech can lead to the death of many others. Rabbi Joseph Telushkin calls such speech "verbal shots." In his book *Jewish Wisdom* (1994), he offers a few valuable sayings that are relevant here. In the Palestinian Talmud (Peah 1:1), it is written: "The gossiper stands in Syria and kills in Rome." Rabbi Leon da Modena (1571–1648) wrote: "Words are the guides to acts; the mouth makes the first move." And Philip Roth writes in *Operation Shylock*: "Lashon hara of such spectacular dimensions that it is guaranteed not only to bring on fear, distress, disease, spiritual isolation, and financial loss but to significantly shorten life. ... No area of your life will go uncontaminated."

Lastly, one of the most haunting Talmudic teachings that comes to my mind on this theme of hatred is the explanation for the destruction of the Second Temple in Jerusalem by the Romans in 70 C.E. We are taught that hatred destroyed the Temple. We are also taught in the Babylonian Talmudic text (Yoma 9b) that while the First Temple (destroyed in 586 B.C.E. by the Babylonians) was rebuilt within 70 years, the Second Temple has never been rebuilt. The sin of hatred is rarely, if ever, acknowledged and thus never repented.

I close with the teaching of the first Ashkenazi Chief Rabbi of Israel, Abraham Isaac Kook, leaving to him the last insight for the antidote to hate: "The Second Temple was destroyed because of causeless hatred. Perhaps the Third will be rebuilt because of causeless love."

Works Cited

Hare, Ivan, and James Weinstein, eds., 2009, Extreme Speech and Democracy, New York: Oxford University Press.

Herz, Michael, and Peter Molnar, eds., 2012, The Content and Context of Hate Speech: Rethinking Regulation and Response, Cambridge: Cambridge University Press.

Holmes, Stephen, 2012, "Waldron, Machiavelli, and Hate Speech," in Michael Herz, and Peter Molnar, eds., The Content and Context of Hate Speech, Cambridge: Cambridge University Press, pp. 345–51.

Telushkin, Joseph, 1994, Jewish Wisdom, New York: Morrow & Co.

Waldron, Jeremy, 2012, The Harm in Hate Speech, Cambridge: Harvard University Press.

CROSSCURRENTS

RENEWED HATE
The Place of Jews and Muslims in Contemporary White Power Thought

C. Richard King

Several years ago, while walking with my daughter to her dance class, we were accosted by a stranger on the street, who berated me for being a Jewish professor. The verbal assault occurred in the wake of an anti-immigration protest held at my university to coincide with an annual event sponsored by a coalition of Latino and indigenous students marking the Day of the Dead. At the same time, some of my faculty were receiving anonymous threats, and it was near the beginning of a several week cycle of leafleting, in which flyers from the National Alliance were hung on doors and bulletin boards around our building at night. While the local police told me not to worry, that my assailant had a screw loose, that he was acting out but was otherwise harmless, the university administration, when pressed, installed a new key-card system to enhance security during evenings and weekends.

Needless to say, these events have left a mark on me, but they also offered valuable lessons about whiteness, anti-Semitism, and evolving attitudes toward racism. These might be summarized as follows: First, white power is an extreme set of ideas, at once something crazy and laughable and a real danger to civic life. Second, freedom of speech covers disrespectful and hateful expressions within institutionally defined zones of permissibility that do not target individuals (in this case, threats online and posting of propaganda). Third, anti-Semitism serves as a flexible center for many advocates of white power, shifting in response to circumstances, adept at creating meaningful objects, lashing out at threats, and anchoring other racial struggles. Fourth, its invocation reveals much more about those who articulate it and their vision of the world than those against whom they wield it.

In the intervening years, as I have increasingly devoted my research to white power, I have returned to the attack and these lessons repeatedly. On the one hand, they reveal the resilience, flexibility, and resurgence of hate, what I have come to think of renewed hate. On the other hand, they have prompted me to be mindful of the relationships between anti-Semitism and other forms of racism animating the political projects and social visions central to such movements and ideologies.

Here, I want to take up the ways in which advocates of white power in the United States represent Muslims and Jews. I unpack their use of anti-Semitism and Islamophobic discourses as well as the relationships between the two in their thought. My reading suggests that whereas these framings render both Muslims and Jews existential threats conspiring to destroy the white race, Islamophobia plays a more supplemental role to anti-Semitism, which remains the dynamic center. My discussion opens with a survey of white power, offering an overview of the evolution and key elements of white power. It then turns to the place of Muslims and Jews in white power discourse.

White power: continuity and change

White power refers to a range of racial ideologies, some of which pretend not to be, and a series of overlapping political movements. These include white supremacism, white separatism, and white nationalism, finding voice in familiar forms like the Ku Klux Klan, the National Alliance, the Aryan Nation, and sundry neo-Nazis, and in less obvious place like neo-Confederates, paleoconservatism, kinism (a Christian-based belief that humanity should organize tribally or along ethnic and racial lines), some variants of paganism, and a range of patriot groups.

White power remains buried in much of U.S. history, an unnamed and largely unnamable phenomenon, a system of racial rule marked by the African slave trade, the expulsion of indigenous people, and the virtual exclusion of non-whites from citizenship. Indeed, white supremacy saturated public culture, intellectual life, and political governance through the Civil War and as recoded in its aftermath up through the Civil Right Movement and the death of Jim Crow. White power, as a social movement and political force distinct from the status quo, or what might be more properly termed white nationalism, had its origins in the Ku Klux Klan and the remnants of the Confederacy, quickened in turned by the eugenics, imperialism, rising nativism, and the rebirth of the KKK in the second decade of the twentieth century. It hardened through its detour through Nazism and return to the United States after the Second World War.

Abby Ferber (1998) has enumerated the key elements of white power in the twentieth century. From her interpretation, such ideologies understand race to be natural, fixed, and essential, constituting a hierarchy of ranked groups. Whites unsurprisingly occupied the pinnacle of this hierarchy racially, culturally, and intellectually. Mixing, in turn, leads to degradation and degeneration, meaning the recognition of and respect for boundaries is crucial to the maintenance of group integrity and identity. Even as these formulations of white power anchored themselves in notions of white supremacy, often explicitly extolling its virtues, advocates lamented the unstable and imperiled conditions of whiteness. Moreover, pronounced anti-black and anti-Indian racisms served as the foundation for such worldviews, supplemented over time by anti-immigrant sentiments and increasingly by anti-Semitism, which would become a key complement to the black/white color line. Importantly, Ferber argues, white power is not just about race, but also about gender and sexuality. As such, it is patriarchal and heteronormative, emphasizing reproduction, sexuality, and the traditional family.

Over the past 50 years, changing social, cultural, and economic conditions have contributed to the reconfiguration of white power. To be overly brief: World War Two exposed the deadly consequences of racial ideologies, while spawning decolonization and the cold war; movements for racial equality, most notably the civil rights movement, ended segregation, challenged the legitimacy of white supremacy, and embraced diversity; overt expressions of racism became increasingly taboo, while multiculturalism emerged as paradigm of inclusion, respect, and recognition; affirmative action and equal opportunity initiatives integrated the work place; and global economic realignments and the success of the second wave of feminism wrought important changes in the status of women and altered gender roles and family structure in the home. Of course, none of these shifts went uncontested, nor have any of them fulfilled their promise. Rather, they have fostered struggle, rethinking, and often retrenchment. Nevertheless, these trends altered how, why, in what forms white power would express itself, prompting important re-articulations.

In response to these changes, advocates of white power have altered the focus, objects, and expressions of their racial ideologies and political projects. In the twenty-first century, one might argue that white power continues to center around race (understanding it to be natural, fixed, and essential), seeks to define and defend boundaries between groups, and positions whites as victims of the state, social mores, and culture industries. Moreover, it is still very much anchored in patriarchy and heteronormativity. It is not, however, universally vested in white supremacy in its crudest formulations. It often favors to speak of love not hate and—borrowing from the success of various freedom struggles—it commonly uses the language of diversity, ethnic nationalism, and identity politics to claim the right to the promotion and preservation of what its advocates see as the unique features of white culture, heritage, and tradition. White power remains anxious, identifying a growing number of threats to its survival and hence a wider array of targets for its resentment and rage. Thus, in the twenty-first century, it has retained its anti-black and anti-Semitic core, but in response to 9/11, the war on terror, demographic shifts, and economic contraction it added immigrants from Latin America and Muslims to its primary pre-occupations and problems.

White power now

Importantly, for over a century, advocates of white power have professed that the world is out of balance, marked by degeneration and chaos. Throughout their writings and speeches, one finds a sense, often expressed with great urgency, that social reconfigurations resulting from globalization, decolonization, civil rights, the rise of multiculturalism, immigration, and post-industrialization have wrought social disintegration and moral decay. In the face of such tumult, they see themselves locked in an existential struggle, variously described as a race war and an ongoing white genocide. In a very real, if perverted way, white power offers a critique of life as lived, but outlines a utopian vision for a better future.

Consequently, white power is a vital and expanding force, driven largely by 9/11 and the subsequent "War on Terror," the election of Obama, and the great recession. In its most recent annual review, the Southern Poverty Law Center (Potok 2014), an organization devoted to monitoring and combatting extremism, offers two key measures of this growth: hate groups in the United States jumped from 457 in 2000 to 939 in 2013, while patriot groups expanded from 158 in 2001 to 1360 in 2012.

The internet and social media have proven key to the rise of extremism generally and white power specifically (Daniels 2009; King and Leonard 2014). In 2011, the Simon Wiesenthal Center identified more than 11,500 websites, forums, blogs, and social networks, including Facebook and YouTube, devoted to hate.[1] These virtual spaces enhance the recruitment of new members and facilitate the construction of communities. They foster the global dissemination of racist ideologies and the mobilization of social actors. The ease of access, ubiquity of connectivity, and the anonymity of participation have all proven central to the success of such media and the growth of white power worldwide.

Representing the other: Muslim and Jew

Advocates of white power routinely reiterate their antipathy toward and anxiety about Muslims and Jews. Among those who care about such things, both are considered to be false religions. More importantly in the movement, however, are racial and cultural issues, evidenced in the distorted and dehumanizing images of both groups. As a result, they rendered both Muslims and Jews as abject others: grotesque, uncivilized, conniving, deviant, and ultimately inhuman. They associate Muslims with violence and religious extremism, consider them to be alien outsider, who refuse to adapt and do not have a capacity to assimilate. They frame many questions with regard to Islam and the West (read whites) in terms on a clash of civilizations. In contrast, they see Jews and Jewish powers everywhere: often borrowing heavily from *The Protocols of the Elders of Zion*, *The International Jew*, and *The Eternal Jew*, they cast them at once as parasites and masterminds, unassimilable outsiders and inside operatives, a flawed people and a transhistorical force, and tribal and cosmopolitan. Thus, whereas Muslims constitute a more singular evil in the minds of many advocates of white power, Jews represent something more nefarious, multi-faceted, and troubling.

Muslims and Jews, then, constitute two of the key problems confronting the movement, rivaled perhaps only by African Americans. Advocates of white power identify each, in distinct ways, as existential threats, understanding each to be participants in a deeper conspiracy against the white race (sometimes glossed more culturally as the West or Western civilization). Thus, Muslims and Jews do not constitute the same sorts of threat or produce the same sort of conspiratorial thinking.

In outlining the Islamic threat, white power advocates use a fairly limited frame, associating the danger with Muslims and their faith in discernible struggles and unfolding conflicts. Their perception of Muslims focuses on intermittent attacks (the French satirical magazine "Charlie Hebdo," for instance) and military actions around the globe. Advocates of white power, like the mainstream media, read these as terrorism and locate their concerns in the Mosque, the sleeper cell, and the insurgent front. They worry about the intrusion of immigrants, infiltration, and conversion (Sharia law in the U.S., recruitment of youth), and the vulnerability of white women. Some have concerns of a government takeover (with Barak Obama's assent) to the Presidency (either by an unspecific Islamic threat or orchestrated by the Muslim Brotherhood). Even though current events pace such theories, this paranoid style often draws upon a history of civilization struggle (the Crusades), and the purported dehumanizing, perverted, and destructive core of the Muslim faith. To round out their Islamophobic vision, they point to the established barbarity of its practitioners. To make sense of Muslims, white power advocates have woven together key elements of Orientalism and the sediments of anti-Islamic thought that crystallized after the Oil Crisis and the Iranian Revolution, grafting this ideological monstrosity onto existing tropes of the immigrant (penetrating alien intent to destroy from within) and the black (violent, sub-human, criminal, inferior).

In contrast to the more limited frame of Islamophobia, for advocates of white power, the so-called Jewish threat knows no bounds. It is transhistorical and transnational. It involves all aspects of life. For many of them, the zeitgeist of history is the struggle of the white race against the machinations of world Jewry. On the one hand, they see Jews controlling every important institution of from the government (which is often referred to as ZOG, the Zionist Occupational Government) and the news media to finance and popular culture. On the other hand, every major crisis (the Great Recession, for instance) or events (like 9/11) can be understood as the work of the Jews, or the Zionists in some circles. Jews act as puppet masters, orchestrating events, and manipulating people, including entire races through welfare (blacks) or entertainment and sports (whites). The purported ultimate goal is the destruction of the white race. The deep anti-Semitism of such narrative and the audible echoes of Nazism in them are inescapable; they distinguish white power ideologies from more acceptable racial ideologies today.

Relational reading: Judeophobia and Islamophobia

The ways advocates of white power use and understand Muslims and Jews vary widely. In fact, the assigned place of each and relations between them within particular political projects is quite revealing. Importantly, while almost all formulations of white power today include anti-Semitic and anti-Islamic sentiments, not all advocates of white power embrace Judeophobia or Islamophobia. These fractures have particularly important implications. What follows is a brief synopsis of the competing positions:

1 *The real enemy is the Muslim:* This unconventional framing of white racial politics finds its clearest expression in *American Renaissance*, a white nationalist website affiliated with the New Century Foundation and run by Jared Taylor. It regularly features pieces with titles like "The Real Threat is Islam" or "The Real Face of Islam." It counts a Jewish astrophysicist as one its leading thinkers. It does not use anti-Semitism to advance its agenda. Importantly, it is among the most centrist in the overt white nationalist movement.

2 *The real enemy is the Jew:* At another extreme, on finds *Vanguard News Network*, a website run by neo-Nazi Alex Linder with the tagline, "No Jews. Just Right." While it does feature articles and discussion forums best described as Islamophobic, its greatest concern—some would say obsession—is what it sees as "the Jewish Problem," featuring an entire series on the subject under the heading "Lox Culture." Significantly, it reads the ongoing race war as first and foremost a "Jewhad," a struggle by Jews against whites; it asserts that this Jewhad paves the way for the more familiar Jihad.

3 *Parallel problems:* Many, perhaps the majority, of white power advocates believe that both Muslims and Jews pose a threat to whites. For instance,

Occidental Dissent, a white nationalist website, recently posted a short piece on the attack on "Charlie Hebdo" as part of the larger danger posed by Islamic terrorism, two days after running a commentary titled, "Jewish Oligarchs Gather to Keep GOP Kosher." Two sources of peril: clear, present, distinct. Importantly, whatever the intentions of the postings, in the comment section on the Paris attacks, participants quickly linked it to and debated a broader Zionist conspiracy.[2]

4 *Racial paranoia: Anti-Semitic obsession and enemies everywhere*: At *Stormfront*, the most popular webforum for the discussion of white nationalism, one finds pronounced racial paranoia: everyone is out to get the white race! Despite this shared sentiments, its discussion threads nicely showcase the conflicting perspectives and cacophony of voices found within the white power sub-culture. Above all else, its members are obsessed with Jewish conspiracies, often mirroring what one finds at *Vanguard News Network* and regularly emphasizing the dangers posed by Islam. Almost invariably, however, when Islam does come up, eventually it is linked to "the Jews." While discussants agree, for instance, that Islam reiterates the dangers of non-white immigration, the deeper danger that should not be missed is Jewish influence that promulgated multiculturalism and cultural Marxism, which softened public sentiment and worked through white politicians to change immigration legislation. At its most extreme, this perspective holds that the threats and attacks associated with radical Islam are part of broader Zionist plan to get the United States to fight their enemies and ultimately weaken and destroy it.

5 *Enemy of my enemy*: Arguably as rare as the rejection of Judeophobia, this position sets aside Islamophobia to advance a plainly anti-Semitic agenda. David Duke, longtime leader of various white power groups, is the chief advocate of this position. He has sought to open dialogue and forge alliances with Islamic leaders, despite the open critique and opposition of others in the white power movement. He believes the two share common goals, namely the destruction of Israel. He has used Holocaust denial and disseminated anti-Israel propaganda and conspiratorial narratives to promote his ends (see Michael 2007).

Thinking comparatively, we can observe key messages underneath such diversity: advocates of white power feel imperiled and disempowered; anti-Islamic and anti-Semitic narratives provide means to recenter a dynamic world around a fixed core (race); these narratives also account for and engage with the world's chaos but can formulate meaningful, if marginalized responses to it.

Conclusion

White power ideologies have identified the Muslim and the Jew as fundamental problems, framing each, often in relation to the other, as a means to articulate racial identity and advance political projects. Importantly, its understandings of Muslims and Jews often run counter to mainstream articulations of racial difference and power. While anti-Semitism has been banished from most aspects of American political discourse, anti-Islamic attitudes appear to be on the rise and even acceptable. This contrasts markedly with white power today, which frequently places Judeophobia at its center, relegating Islamophobia to a more marginal position. In fact, those variations of white nationalism closest to the mainstream tend to reject anti-Semitism and, instead, amplify anti-Islamist elements, an approach that mirrors the formulations and pre-occupations of a range of rightist political programs since 9/11.

Notes

1. Simon Wiesenthal Center, "iReport: Online Terror + Hate the First Decade," www.wiesenthal.com/atf/cf/%7BDFD2AAC1-2ADE-428A-9263-35234229D8D8%7D/IREPORT.PDF
2. Anti-Defamation League, "Anti-Semitic Conspiracies Predictably Surface after Paris Attacks. ADL Blog, http://blog.adl.org/international/anti-semitic-conspiracies-after-paris-attacks (accessed 9 January 2015).

Works Cited

Daniels, Jessie, 2009, Cyber Racism: White Supremacy Online and the New Attack on Civil Rights, Lanham, MD: Rowman and Littlefield.

Ferber, Abby L., 1998, White Man Falling: Race, Gender, and White Supremacy, Lanham, MD: Rowman and Littlefield.

King, C. Richard, and David J. Leonard, 2014, Beyond Hate: White Power and Popular Culture, Burlington, VT: Ashgate.

Michael, George, 2007, "Deciphering Ahmadinejad's Holocaust Revisionism," Middle East Quarterly **14**(3), pp. 11–8.

Potok, Mark, 2014, "The Year in Hate and Extremism," Intelligence Report (Spring), www.splcenter.org/get-informed/intelligence-report/browse-all-issues/2014/spring/The-Year-in-Hate-and-Extremism.

CROSSCURRENTS

MAKING ENEMIES: THE USES AND ABUSES OF TAINTED IDENTITIES

Alex Alvarez

After the terrorist attacks of September 11, 2001, rumors began spreading that no Jews had died on that fateful day at the World Trade Center because the Mossad—the Israeli Intelligence Agency—had forewarned Jews who worked there to stay at home. According to this theory, the state of Israel was behind the attacks in order to force the United States to attack the enemies of Israel.[1] In reality, it is estimated that there were approximately 300 to 400 Jews who were killed at the World Trade Center when the buildings collapsed after the hijacked airliners crashed into them. After the economic recession began in 2008, various rumors began spreading that Jewish bankers were largely responsible for the meltdown. One story asserted that the Lehman Brothers Investment firm sent $400 million dollars to Israel just before declaring bankruptcy in the largest such filing in American history and one which had deep repercussions throughout the world economy. It was also during this period that the scandal involving Bernie Madoff's Ponzi scheme erupted and much was made of his Jewishness. More recently, in 2014 the conflict in Gaza resulted in an upsurge of anti-Semitic rhetoric and attacks throughout Europe and the United States.[2] From a shooting at a Jewish museum in Brussels, Belgium, to the firebombing of a synagogue in Wuppertal, Germany, the summer of 2014 saw a sharp increase in this kind of hate-based violence. Clearly, anti-Semitism is alive and well in the twenty-first century. So much so, in fact, that in January 2015 the United Nations hosted its first-ever meeting dedicated to fighting anti-Semitism worldwide,[3] while on January 27, 2015, the president of the World Jewish Congress spoke on the seventieth anniversary of the liberation of Auschwitz and summarized the present-day situation thusly: "For a time, we thought that the hatred of the Jews had finally been eradicated. But slowly the demonization of Jews started to come back. Once again, young Jewish boys are afraid to wear yarmulkes on the streets of Paris and Budapest and London. Once again, Jewish businesses are targeted. And once again, Jewish families are fleeing Europe."[4]

Why is this the case? Why has anti-Semitism persisted over such a long period of time? Anti-Semitism actually predates Christianity, yet this ancient form of intolerance continues to crop up with alarming regularity in modern times (see, for example, Wistrich 2010). What is it about these ideas that are so resilient and enduring? While there is no single or simple answer to these questions, there do appear to be a number of issues that are important for keeping not only this particular form of prejudice alive, but other similar forms of bigotry as well. Parts of the answer lie in the deep-seated predisposition humans have to see the world in binary terms: us vs. them. We instinctively tend to identify with and prefer those individuals that are similar to us, or as the political scientist Kristen Renwick Monroe asserts, "even putting aside differences in social standing, economic and political power, or culture, in-group favoritism is a powerful force in human behavior" (Monroe 2012, 18). Crucially, this natural inclination also involves a process of comparison between groups that usually involves hierarchically ordering the in-group versus the out-group, or as Monroe further points out, "As part of this process, we compare our in-groups with other groups, and find a favorable bias toward the group to which we belong. Social Identity theory thus roots prejudice, discrimination, and the violence that can result from it in an innate psychological need for distinctiveness" (19). In-group solidarity is strengthened by such disparaging sentiments since it confirms one's own group as being superior to others. This cohesion and sense of belonging is also strengthened by conflict since it encourages members to unite against a common enemy. Such differentiation has the added impact of making it easier to harm members of out-groups since it removes or diminishes moral or normative prohibitions against harming others. We reserve our concern and restraint for those who belong to our group: people who we identify with. The sociologist Helen Fein puts it best when she describes how this process of differentiation serves to remove people from membership in certain communities and thereby places them outside of the "universe of obligation" (Fein 1993). Members of out-groups, in other words, are generally perceived as being inferior and because of this are more easily stereotyped, scapegoated, and stigmatized. Furthermore, defining a person as a lesser form of life makes it easier to discriminate against, harm, and kill members of that group since it doesn't call forth the same emotional response and empathy that killing someone like us would stimulate.

Human beings, in short, have a predisposition to engage in the kinds of thinking that produces anti-Semitism and similar kinds of out-group hatred. To define the "Jew," the Bosnian Muslim, or the Rwandan Tutsi as the "other" is to deprive them of their identity as individuals, neighbors, fellow citizens, and even as human beings. It demarcates them as being different from the other "normal" members of a society and stigmatizes them.

Stigma refers to a situation in which a person's identity and behavior are tainted because of certain perceived defects in their character or because they belong to some vilified group. To anti-Semites, the Jews shared certain ascribed qualities and characteristics that superseded all other identifying qualities and characteristics. This becomes especially salient when we understand that out of this tendency to differentiate and denigrate, stereotypes arise describing and highlighting certain characteristics that all members of the out-group are purported to share. Unfortunately, these ascribed qualities tend not to be rooted in fact, behavior, and reality, but are all too often entrenched in profound ignorance. Anti-Semitism, for example, "has very little to do with the actual behavior of Jews or the strictures of their highly ethical religion," but is instead based on "delusionary perceptions that are accepted as authoritative and passed on and embellished from generation to generation" (Perry and Schweitzer 2002, 3). The power of these prejudices is often magnified when the bias becomes intertwined with nationalist mythologies, religious beliefs, racial and ethnic phobias, and xenophobic ideologies. Furthermore, these mythological attributes often create a self-fulfilling prophecy since everything that person does is interpreted in light of that all-encompassing label. It doesn't matter what members of that group may say or do, their actions and words are defined and understood through the lens of the stereotype.

Psychologists have long known that human beings tend to observe the world selectively and focus on those behaviors that reinforce preexisting opinions and ignore those that contradict them. To the anti-Semite, a Jew in Germany was always a Jew, no matter how well assimilated Jews were. Much evidence also suggests that these stereotypes are highly resilient and resistant to change (Rothbart 1981). Once established, these ideologies of discrimination may wax and wane, but they never completely go away; given the right circumstances they can provide a potent weapon for those unscrupulous enough to utilize them. This is why systems of thought devaluing other groups (of which anti-Semitism is a preeminent example) have often helped facilitate the pursuit of certain social, political, and/or economic goals. Hatred and prejudice have been effective tools exploited by political, social, and religious leaders seeking to achieve some objective, mobilize populations, or deflect attention from other issues.

We see the perverse usefulness of prejudice and bias most clearly when we examine the ways in which they have often been instrumental in enabling the perpetration of mass atrocity crimes, such as genocide. To understand this relationship, it is important to first appreciate that genocide and similar forms of mass atrocity crimes do not just happen, but instead require a great deal of planning, organization, and logistical preparation. Because of this, they are often much more intentional than commonly believed. One common trope about genocide is that they are the result of ancient tribal and ethnic hatreds boiling over and erupting into exterminatory violence. This, however, is a false and misleading perception (Alvarez 2001). The unfortunate truth is that certain types of states all too often view policies of extermination as rational and even desirable methods for accomplishing specific ambitions. Writing about ethnic cleansing, the political scientist Martin Naimark suggests that "ethnic cleansing as experienced in former Yugoslavia... is a profoundly modern experience, related to previous instances in the twentieth century but not a product of 'ancient hatreds'" (Naimark 2001, 10). This reality is further supported by Chris Hedges who, in his book, *War is a Force that Gives Meaning*, writes that "the ethnic conflicts and insurgencies of our time, whether between Serbs and Muslims or Hutus and Tutsis are not religious wars. They are not clashes between cultures or civilizations, nor are they the result of ancient ethnic hatreds. They are manufactured wars, born out of the collapse of civil societies" (Hedges 2002, 20). In other words, what Hedges and Naimark point out is that social, political, and religious leaders sometimes make conscious choices to foster intergroup conflict when it suits their needs. In short, genocides are perpetrated with the specific determination to destroy targeted populations and represent conscious strategies in pursuit of an assortment of goals that can involve ideological belief systems, economic imperatives, a desire to maintain power during a crisis or war situation, and/or retribution for real or perceived historic injustices (Fein 1993). While these motivations can vary depending on the specific case, they nevertheless almost invariably depend upon political leaders successfully generating popular support for policies that target certain groups for removal or elimination, and this reality has important ramifications for systems of intolerance and prejudice as exemplified by anti-Semitism.

History has shown that decision makers have often used popular prejudices to help facilitate their ambitions. In Germany, it was about the Nazi struggle for political power during the Weimar years and their pursuit of utopian ideals of nation and race (see Weitz 2003). In Bosnia, it was about the dissolution of the former Yugoslavia and the desire to create a Greater Serbia (Sell 2002), while in Rwanda it was about the extremist government losing a civil war and seeking to maintain power (Des Forges 1999). In each case, popular support, cooperation, and participation were harnessed and mobilized by the conscious manipulation of historic ethnic prejudice and intolerance. The historic nature of these bigotries is important to emphasize the following: They provide a narrative that is easy to access since they tap into preexisting ideas and images that many, if not most, within that society are acquainted with. In fact, as Ervin Staub points out, "A history of devaluation of a group, negative stereotypes, and negative images perpetuated in the products of the culture, its literature, art, and media 'preselects' this group as a potential scapegoat and enemy" (Staub 2002, 15).

It should be noted, however, that to a certain degree, these have often been resurrected antagonisms. In Germany during the early part of the twentieth century, for example, Jews were well assimilated into society and much of the historic antipathy against them appeared to have ebbed into relative insignificance (Graml 1992). While pockets and undercurrents of active anti-Semitism persisted and periodically flared back into renewed vigor, by and large, German Jews and gentiles lived together, worked together, sometimes intermarried, and outwardly appeared to have achieved amity. The same was true for Rwandan Hutu and Tutsi, and Bosnian Muslim and Serb, in the years leading up to those respective genocides (Rwanda in 1994 and Bosnia between 1992 and 1995). In each of these cases, however, the historic antagonisms were consciously revitalized and deployed in service to specific goals and thereby gained a powerful and destructive new relevance.

In many ways, this kind of intentional manipulation builds upon human nature. During difficulty social, economic, and/or political times—when people and communities feel threatened, besieged, and scared—popular attitudes harden and become much more punitive especially in regard to those who are perceived as being outsiders and different (Costelloe *et al.* 2007). These exclusionary and punitive sentiments often revolve around those groups that have experienced a previous history of antagonism and persecution. They provide a ready-made victim group to scapegoat and blame. It's easy to see how during tough times old antipathies can spring back into life and then be fostered, manipulated, and employed by those with specific political, economic, social, and religious agendas. In their pursuit of political power, for example, the Nazis relied upon anti-Semitism to provide a convenient focus for the fear, anger, bitterness, and resentment felt by many Germans and proved a useful tool for campaign rallies and speeches. Even though many ordinary Germans did not necessarily know any Jews personally or have strong anti-Semitic feelings, they were nevertheless familiar with many of the anti-Semitic stereotypes that were such a long-standing and widespread part of European history. When the Nazis used these ideas to scapegoat the Jews for the German loss of the First World War (the so-called stab-in-the-back-legend), the failings of the Weimar Government, the rise of Communism, political violence and revolution in many German cities, and the Great Depression, they were relying on messages whose themes were very familiar to Germans, even if any particular individual didn't actively subscribe to them (Evans 2004). Persecution of the Jews was not just perpetrated by active anti-Semites, but was also enabled by many thousands of others who passively accepted the revitalized anti-Semitic prejudices that were used to justify discrimination and oppression. It was a great deal easier to blame the Jews, for example, than the impersonal and confusing economic forces that led to the

Great Depression. Because of the deeply embedded history of anti-Semitism, the Nazis were able to effectively scapegoat the Jews using ideas that tapped into a preexisting and deep reservoir of prejudice.

The same kind of process occurred in Turkey, Rwanda, and Bosnia in the months and years leading up to genocide in those respective locations (see, for example, Kiernan 2009). Importantly, in each country a previous legacy of intolerance, prejudice, hate, and persecution served to create a substratum of prejudice that could be resurrected, manipulated, and used at opportune times; these resurrected antagonisms provided a vehicle that lent credibility to certain groups, actions, and behaviors and scapegoated, delegitimized, and made vulnerable those targeted by these systems of hatred. The mere fact that these prejudices have a long existence confers a sense of legitimacy on them by virtue of having endured for a long period of time. Michael Ignatieff describes this beautifully when he writes, "it is not how the past dictates to the present but how the present manipulates the past that is decisive" (Ignatieff 1995, 22). Max Weber, in his classic work on authority, famously suggested that legitimacy is often conferred simply on the basis of tradition and custom, and this is certainly the case with anti-Semitism (Weber 1978).

The argument as to the utility of prejudice is not to suggest that those fanning the flames of intolerance do not share the destructive sentiments that they manipulate and use. In point of fact, Adolf Hitler and many Nazis were virulent anti-Semites who believed deeply in the myths and stereotypes that they were peddling to the German people. To the Nazis, the Jews represented an existential threat to the Aryan race and were responsible for all sorts of outrages, some more fanciful than the next. Acknowledging this reality, however, does not take away from the fact that these attitudes and beliefs were also consciously exploited for political gain. It also did not hurt that Jews represented only a very small percentage of the German population. The historian Laurence Rees frames this nicely when he writes that "from Hitler's perspective – the Jews were an extremely useful enemy. The vast majority of Germans knew they were not Jews and so were relatively safe from persecution. For a charismatic leader like Hitler, the more there is one single enemy for propaganda to focus upon and the more that enemy is a clearly defined minority from which the vast bulk of the population know they are excluded, the better" (Rees 2012, 110).

In many ways, the exploitation of discriminatory ideologies, such as anti-Semitism, involves a process of scapegoating in which a person or group is identified as being responsible for the problems facing a society. It typically involves a community focusing their animus against a person or group that embodies the "other" and which have a long history of previous prejudice and discrimination. Sometimes it is a tool to deflect blame and criticism, while at other times it provides easily understood and emotionally satisfying answers to difficult issues for which the true causes may be hard to understand and/or emotionally unsatisfying. Many Germans, for example, found it hard to comprehend why they had lost the First World War, especially since their armies were still in the trenches. Likewise, understanding the impersonal and complicated economic forces that caused the great depression proved difficult to fathom for many people not versed in economics and did not resonate on an emotional level. Who can you direct your anger against and blame when standard explanations focus on impersonal market forces, stock markets, commodities, and bank failure? Hence, when the Nazis blamed Jewish profiteers and bankers for Germany's military loss in the First World War and the economic collapse in 1929, their argument built upon long-standing biases that provided a focal point for the fear, anger, and frustration felt by many within Germany.

This was nothing new. Far from it. During the Middle Ages, the causes of plague were not understood and scientific principles concerning germs and viruses, pandemics, disease vectors, and contagion were as yet unknown. When Jews were tortured into confessing that they had poisoned wells on the orders of their rabbis, this was an explanation that made sense to ordinary folks because it provided an enemy to vilify and closely aligned with the preexisting images of Jews as being an enemy. It was also no accident that those most vociferous in scapegoating the Jews were often those most in debt to Jewish moneylenders. Even in those times, those who stood to gain the most often exploited anti-Semitism.

Anti-Semitism has persisted for a very long period of time and remains a persistent threat even in these modern times. Its longevity can be attributed to the fact that it is rooted in certain deep-seated human tendencies to identify with those nearest to us and to differentiate ourselves from those who are different. Its tenacity can be further explained by its usefulness to those willing to exploit bias and prejudice in pursuit of contemporary goals and agendas. Until these underlying forces can be comprehensively addressed, systems of thought such as anti-Semitism will continue to flourish and haunt this world.

Notes

1. Anti-Defamation League, 2003, *Unraveling Anti-Semitic 9/11 Conspiracy Theories*, New York: Gorowitz Institute.
2. For a detailed review of anti-Semitic events in the United States and Europe, see the Anti-Defamation League website at www.adl.org.
3. Time Staff, "U.N. Hosts First Ever Meeting Dedicated to Combating Anti-Semitism," *Time Magazine*, January 23, 2015 (accessed January 24, 2015, http://time.com/3679744/united-nations-u-n-anti-semitism-islamophobia/?xid=newsletter-brief).
4. Cited in Vanessa Gera, 2015, "On Auschwitz Anniversary, Leader Warns Jews Again Targets," *Azdailysun.com*, January 27 (accessed January 28, 2015, http://azdailysun.com/news/-world/europe/on-auschwitz-anniversary-leader-warns-jews-again-targets/article_e4a269dc-778d-5c67-b1a2-1d4832f5825f.html).

Works Cited

Alvarez, Alex, 2001, Governments, Citizens, and Genocide: A Comparative and Interdisciplinary Approach, Bloomington, IN: Indiana University Press.

Costelloe, Michael, Ted Chiricos, and Marc Gertz, 2007, "Punitive Attitudes Toward Criminals: Exploring the Relevance of Crime Salience and Economic Insecurity," Punishment and Society **11**, pp. 25–49.

Des Forges, Alison, 1999, Leave None to Tell the Story: Genocide in Rwanda, New York: Human Rights Watch.

Evans, Richard J., 2004, The Coming of the Third Reich, New York: The Penguin Press.

Fein, Helen Fein, 1993, Genocide: A Sociological Perspective, London: Sage.

Graml, Hermann, 1992, Antisemitism in the Third Reich, Oxford: Blackwell Wiley.

Hedges, Chris, 2002, War is a Force That Gives Us Meaning, New York: Anchor Books.

Ignatieff, Michael, 1995, Blood and Belonging: Journeys Into the New Nationalism, New York: Farrar, Straus, and Giroux.

Kiernan, Ben, 2009, Blood and Soil: A World History of Genocide and Extermination From Sparta to Darfur, New Haven: Yale University Press.

Monroe, Kristen Renwick, 2012, Ethics in an Age of Terror and Genocide: Identity and Moral Choice, Princeton: Princeton University Press.

Naimark, Norman M., 2001, Fires of Hatred: Ethnic Cleansing in the Twentieth-Century Europe, Cambridge: Harvard University Press.

Perry, Marvin, and Frederick M. Schweitzer, 2002, Antisemitism: Myth and Hate From Antiquity to the Present, New York: Palgrave Macmillan.

Rees, Laurence, 2012, Hitler's Charisma: Leading Millions Into the Abyss, New York: Pantheon Books.

Rothbart, Myron, 1981, "Memory Processes and Social Beliefs", in David L. Hamilton, ed., Cognitive Processes in Stereotyping and Intergroup Behavior, Hillsdale, NJ: Lawrence Erlbaum Associates, pp. 145–82.

Sell, Louise, 2002, Slobodan Milosevic and the Destruction of Yugoslavia, Durham: Duke University Press.

Staub, Ervin, 2002, "The Psychology of Bystanders, Perpetrators, and Heroic Helpers," in Leonard S. Newman, and Ralph Erber, eds., Understanding Genocide: The Social Psychology of the Holocaust, New York: Oxford University Press, pp. 11–42.

Weber, Max, 1978, "An Outline of Interpretive Sociology, Chapter X", in Guenther Roth, and Claus Wittich, eds., Economy and Society, Berkeley: University of California Press, pp. 941–55.

Weitz, Eric D., 2003, A Century of Genocide: Utopias of Race and Nation, Princeton: Princeton University Press.

Wistrich, Robert S., 2010, A Lethal Obsession: Anti-Semitism From Antiquity to the Global Jihad, New York: Random House.

CROSSCURRENTS

ISLAMOPHOBIA AND ANTI-SEMITISM
Shared Prejudice or Singular Social Pathologies

Michael Dobkowski

There is no doubt: there has been a significant rise in anti-Semitism and Islamophobia in recent years. Both have deep roots in history as well as being generated by more recent political and economic influences. Some see them as basically parallel phenomena, characterized more by their similarities than their differences. Others believe that anti-Semitism is a unique prejudice that really stands alone and cannot be compared to Islamophobia or even racism. What I will attempt to do in this essay is to provide a theoretical and historical framework for approaching this complex and controversial question. I don't expect my analysis will satisfy everyone, but I do hope it will generate additional thinking on these impactful "hatreds."

The roots of Islamophobia

Let me briefly begin with some context. Islamophobia is a term first put into use in 1997 in a report of the Runnymede Trust, a think tank in Britain launched by the British Home Secretary Jack Straw. It was given further currency by the 2001 UN conference on racism at Durban that most observers believe devolved from an examination of racism to an exercise in racism and anti-Semitism. Israel was singled out for special criticism prompting the U.S. delegates to walk out. The official declarations eventually included a reference to anti-Semitism, but this was counterbalanced by the addition of Islamophobia suggesting an equivalency between the two phenomena. Clearly, Muslim populations around the world are experiencing a hostile pressure and waves of discrimination that come from non-Muslim populations of various sorts—the product of Hindu–Muslim tensions in India, of Christian–Muslim competition in Africa, of Jewish–Arab disputes in Israel and Palestine, and of anti-Muslim immigrant sentiment in Europe and North America. There have been countless incidents of stereotyping, scapegoating, and bigotry directed against Muslims because of their religious identity. There exists a huge and profound ignorance about Islam. There is no shortage of voices proclaiming that fanaticism and intolerance are fundamental to Islamic tradition, that horrific violence against enemies of Islam and people defined as infidels have deep Qur'anic roots (Yoffie 2011, 121). Many believe and are spreading the image that Islam is the enemy of the West, America, and Israel and that it is a religion prone to violence and terrorism. This tendency is certainly fueled by a long tradition of anti-Muslim discourse in Western history and culture—from Dante to Don Quixote, to basic Orientalist scholarship; it has been exacerbated by ignorance, bigotry, and post-9/11 fears. Islamophobia is real and to a certain extent is ingrained in Western culture. In his *Orientalism*, Edward Said demonstrated that the West's reified view of Islam has its roots in European colonialism. In his *Covering Islam*, he showed how these colonial notions continue to influence Western coverage of the Middle East in the 1990s. Islamophobia needs to be examined and confronted. It results from ignorance and from limited social contact, which is in turn buttressed by conflict and violence occurring around the world and its treatment by mainstream culture. This anxiety, like most prejudices, relies on a sense of otherness (Mattson 2011, 129–130).

Similarly, anti-Semitism remains a persistent prejudice. The murder of Jewish shoppers at the Parisian Hyper Casher supermarket on January 9, 2015, after the killing of twelve people at the offices of the satirical magazine Charlie Hebdo on January 7, was particularly disturbing, not because it was the first such event but because it has become part of a troubling pattern. By every measure, there has been a rise of anti-Semitism around the world—incidents of violence and intimidation, negative polling data, incitement, desecrations, rhetoric, etc. In 2006, Ilan Halimi was kidnapped, tortured, and murdered in Paris. In 2012, Mehdi Nemmouche killed four people at the Jewish museum in Brussels. In 2012, a rabbi and three young children were murdered at a Jewish school in Toulouse by Mohammad Merah. In early February 2015, there were killings in Copenhagen, and 300 Jewish graves were desecrated in Eastern France. Additionally, there were smaller affronts like the popularity of the *quenelle* gesture (a reverse Nazi salute created by a controversial but widely appreciated French comedian), compounded by attacks on visibly identifiable Jews and anti-Israel protests during the summer's Gaza war devolving into anti-Semitism with marchers shouting anti-Semitic epithets such as, "Juif, la France n'est pas a toi" (Jew, France is not yours).

What is fueling this resurgence? At this point in history, anti-Semitism has become so embedded in the subterranean history and mythology of hatred that it provides a template for whatever hurts need to find a simple-minded balm: the Jews are responsible. It is being stimulated by the sympathetic response that many Muslims in Europe have to the plight of the Palestinians, stimulated by the Gaza war and the transformation of an essentially political conflict into something more sinister and even religious in nature; by the symptoms of economic and social disadvantage; and by the failures of an immigration and assimilation policy that has created a two tier European society with millions of disaffected Muslims. It is stirred by the rise of radical Islam that has defined the principle enemies of Islam to be the West, Zionist Israel, blasphemers, and Jews. For the global jihadists, Israel and the Jews are perceived as an existential threat to Muslim culture and collective identity. Israel is theologically and ontologically intolerable because it exercises authority over sacred Muslim territory. Global conspiracy theories abound in jihadist literature and thinking repreiving apocalyptic themes reminiscent of medieval Christian and twentieth-century Nazi ideologies blaming Jews for the suffering in the Muslim world.

People are afraid and anxious, and in that state, they often look for scapegoats, be they Muslims or Jews. Throughout history, anti-Semitism has been the weapon of choice for demagogues, for ideologically driven extremists, and, as Jean-Paul Sartre has argued, for people attracted to a Manichaen, dualistic worldview, for it helps deflect the complaints of the disaffected away from the real causes of their misery (Sartre 1965). We are seeing that play out again in Europe and other parts of the world. On the right of Europe's political spectrum, anger is rising against Islam, against marginalized Muslim communities who in turn feel discriminated against and misrepresented with cause. The past provides a reserve of reference, symbols, and ideas for the present, but it does not explain it. The

Ottoman siege of Vienna in 1683 or the Crusades do not explain current tensions. Muslim grievances have much more to do with injustices unleashed by colonialism, the failure to integrate new immigrants, the stifling of their complaints, the pressure on school curricula, dress, prayer, and religious observance, and finally the West's demonization of Muslims because of suspicions real or imagined. That largely explains, along with the perverted moral agency of the Islamist quest, why several thousand young European Muslims are joining the forces of ISIS and other radical Islamist groups. Europe's Jews are also on edge with reason.

Exclusionary prejudice vs. ideological prejudice

We know that there are underlying causes that stimulate anti-Semitism and Islamophobia. People who have grievances have a cognitive opening to prejudice and are vulnerable. Are we dealing with mirror image hatreds or with social pathologies that fundamentally are different in origin, characteristics, intensity, pervasiveness, and lethality? There certainly is a prevailing attitude that claims that prejudice, whatever its ostensible target, is basically the same in nature and in causation. The underlying idea is that the essence of prejudice is exclusion, with the goal of privileging a certain group against the discriminated one. According to this theory, racism works to sustain white power structures by excluding black and brown people; sexism sustains male power structures; elitism excludes those who fail to meet the arbitrary standards that define cultural elites and so on. Prejudice exists because there exists a rational motive for people to be prejudiced, namely the maintenance of power structures, economic advantage, and status.

From this perspective, anti-Semitism is just one more form of racism and is not fundamentally distinguishable from Islamophobia. The targets are different, but their essences are not. I believe that this conceptualization is actually misleading and for the most part incorrect. Obviously, anti-Semitism shares some characteristics with Islamophobia and more generally with racism, but in most ways it eclipses the conceptual boundaries of other hatreds and stands apart from them (Harrison 2013, 10–14).

As mentioned earlier, most of what we label racism, sexism, Islamophobia, and so on is probably best classified as social or exclusionary prejudice. It seeks the exclusion of the identified groups and seeks to achieve that aim largely by stereotyping. One thing to say about stereotypes is that there usually is some element of truth to them—there are some materialistic Jews with a special talent to make money, or some criminally inclined African Americans, or some violent Muslims, or some stingy Dutch people, and so on. It is also clear that there are many members of the targeted groups who don't conform to the stereotype and there are also many people who conform exactly to it but who are not members of that group. The other salient point about exclusionary prejudice is that irrational fear, except when it involves criminality or violence, plays a minor role in it (Harrison 2013, 15–16).

The roots of anti-Semitism
Anti-Semitism, however, is an even more sinister form of prejudice because it is characterized by irrational fear, a fear that springs largely from the belief that Jews are a mysterious and depraved people interested in domination. Anti-Semites claim that because of the conspiratorial nature of Jewish culture and its power to extend its influence throughout the social fabric of non-Jewish society, Jews constitute a permanent threat to the well-being of any society that includes them. And this notion of Jewish domination and cultural infiltration has a long history in Western tradition. David Nirenberg (2013) argues cogently in *Anti-Judaism: The Western Tradition* that the idea of Judaism that bears only a passing resemblance to Judaism as practiced and lived by Jews has been at the center of Western civilization since the beginning. From Ptolemaic Egypt to early Christianity, from the Catholic Middle Ages to the Protestant Reformation, from the Enlightenment to Nazism, whenever the West has wanted to define everything it is not—when it wants to put a name to its deepest fears and irrational aversions—the Jew and Judaism has been the "concept" that comes most easily to mind. A version of this tendency is prevalent in certain strains of Muslim fundamentalism that is not marginal or unusual, particularly in the Arab–Muslim world. Jews are described as malevolent, as the enemies of the Prophet, rejecters of Allah's truth, dishonest, and conspirators against Islam (Berman 2003).

The roots of these negative ideas that characterize the "Jew" as sinister, parasitic, cunning, conspiratorial, corrupting, and so on lie in antiquity, especially the early Christian polemic against Judaism. If anti-Semitism is not the longest hated, it is certainly the most resilient. Over the centuries, the stereotype became detached from its religious moorings. It was secularized after the enlightenment in the racial doctrines of Richard Wagner, Huston Stuart Chamberlain, Karl Lueger, and others that mythologized "the Jew" as a demonic, eternal source of evil. This racial and ideological anti-Semitism reached its logical apex in genocidal Nazism and then moved on in the postwar era, when the creation of the State of Israel provided a new target for old obsessions. Robert Wistrich (2010), Daniel Jonah Goldhagen (2013), and others have demonstrated the remarkable persistence and essential continuity of anti-Semitism from its ancient origins to today. Through all its permutations, there has been a consistent parade of delusions and hallucinations about the corrupting omnipresence of Jews that would be dismissed as comical if they did not have such a murderous history associated with them.

What makes anti-Semitism distinctive is that it is a worldview, a means of explaining why there is injustice, unfairness, and conflict in our societies. It is a worldview driven by irrational fear that really has very little to do with objective conditions, lived situations, or Jews for that matter. It is part of a culture of hatred and fear that has over two millennia produced an almost unfathomable reservoir of dehumanization of the Jews. These irrational anti-Semitic tropes include the charge of deicide, the desecration of God's body (the host), the attempt to kill God's prophet (Muhammed), the ritual murder of Christian children to use their blood for baking Matzoh, the poisoning of wells and the Black Death, witchcraft, and conspiring to destroy Christendom and Islam. In modern times, Jews are accused of creating financial havoc and causing wars so they can control societies, for corrupting the moral fabric of society and sexual licentiousness and for the promotion of revolutionary socialist ideologies as well as the predations of capitalism. Jews control the media and through the machinations of Zionism and their influence in Washington they are a vanguard of the West to subjugate Muslims and destroy Islam. Again, what is particularly striking is the deeply irrational and counterfactual character of most accusations that have been leveled against Jews during the past two thousand years (Wistrich 2010, 8–76; Goldhagen 2013, 3–11).

The longevity of anti-Semitism and its reach are just two indications of its sui generis nature. Hundreds of millions of people have, in the past and today, subscribed to the foundational anti-Semitic paradigms. But a more telling phenomenological difference is its irrational nature. There is not a shred of truth to any of these accusations. In this, they are very different from the kinds of stereotypes that fuel exclusionary prejudice that may have some small basis in reality. It has not been a mere reflex response to the differences of the targeted group, to their alleged negative traits or a visceral dislike that ultimately is what drives most exclusionary prejudices like Islamophobia. With anti-Semitism, it is impossible to match the prejudice of irrational fear with reality. The "Jewish conspiracy" has no members (Harrison 2013, 16).

In social and historical terms, anyone familiar with Jewish history and communal life would find ridiculous the claim of a single or even a common purpose there (two Jews and three opinions). Since there has been no central or coordinated authority in the 2,000 years of post-exile Judaism, it is difficult to understand what a claim to a common Jewish identity or purpose would even mean. The idea that a widely scattered nation that never exceeded twenty million people and now hovers around eleven million could conceivably elaborate and by secret machinations "control" vast and powerful nations, manipulate world economies, and destabilize a world order, is an absurd and paranoid fantasy. The ritual murderers and consumers of Christian blood never existed. The actual content of this prejudice of fear belongs in the same category as belief in UFO's, that Elvis still lives, or that Big Foot roams the forests of the Northwest. The only problem is that irrational anti-Semitic fear has led to unspeakable atrocities, even genocide, and the belief systems it has created in susceptible minds are real enough.

One can get a good sense of the inner landscape of such a mind by reading the French existentialist philosopher, Jean-Paul Sartre's *Anti-Semite and Jew*. It had great influence on intellectuals in the West and contains ideas that even today sound remarkably prescient. Anti-Semitism, he claims, is not merely an idea. "It is first of all a passion," and this predisposition is not caused by experience. "Far from experience producing his idea of the Jew, it was the latter which explained his experience. If the Jew did not exist, the anti-Semite would invent him" (Sartre 1965, 13).

At its core, anti-Semitism is a form of Manichaeism, a dualistic worldview that surmised a relentless either-or-struggle between the principles of good and evil. "Between these two principles no reconciliation is conceivable; one of them must triumph and the other annihilated... The Jew is everywhere, the earth is lost, it is up to the Aryan," the anti-Semite believes, "never to compromise, never to make peace" (Sartre 1965, 40–41).

For Sartre, the anti-Semite "localizes all the evil of the universe in the Jew. If nations war with each other...it is because the Jew is there behind the governments, breathing discord. If there is class struggle...it is because Jewish demagogues...have seduced the workers." Manichaeism is not some rationalization for prejudice. "It is the original choice of Manichaeism which explains and conditions anti-Semitism" (Sartre 1965, 40–41).

Sartre's theory cogently argues that the object of the prejudice of irrational fear, as distinct from exclusionary and social prejudice, is not the individual but the group, and the stakes are very high. There is no compromising, even with "Jews of good will," because such compromise, probably impossible anyway, would detract from the ultimate goal of eliminating evil in the world. "Knight-errant of the Good, the anti-Semite is a holy man... Thus the conflict is raised to a religious plane and the end of the combat can be nothing other than a holy destruction" (Sartre 1965, 43). The anti-Semite's terror, his sense that the "Jew is everywhere," is not prompted by anything the Jew does or even any experience with the Jew, but by the "idea" of the Jew, by the Jewish collectivity. And that it is why anti-Semitism has been so enduring and difficult to eradicate and why, possibly, it reached a genocidal extreme. People do not engage in a campaign of genocide against a group because they disapprove of certain characteristics or consider them a nuisance. They do so only when they can be brought to believe the group in question is in fact a collectivity and is characterized by an "idea" that is unparalleled in its evil and intent. The Nazis undertook the Holocaust because they were deeply convinced that it was the right thing to do in order to purify the world of Jews whom they considered the most diabolical threat to decency and justice. Their beliefs justified their actions. The anti-Semitic "idea" of the Jew in itself—is reason enough to despise Jews.

When we look at Islamophobia, in contrast, we see something very different. We observe a fear of a religion that currently has approximately one and half billion adherents, that is the majority faith in dozens of nation states and that has shown the capacity (as state and non-state actors) to engage in violence and terrorism. Is it reasonable; is it rational to fear some Muslims, especially those who are violent and extremist?

There are many people who have real reason to fear violence aimed at them from within the Muslim world and in the name of Islam. Of course, the overwhelming majority of victims of Muslim violence are Muslims so clearly none of this justifies the fear, and even less so the hatred, directed at Muslims, in general or any other expression of prejudice or discrimination. But there is some rational basis to it.

Phobia means a fear or hatred, or some mixture of these and similar feelings like aversion, antipathy, and so on. Phobias are not necessarily active. Many people have phobias and never act upon them. Anti-Semitism, in contrast, implies being against Jews and even the term suggests action. Being anti-something means being opposed to it (Yakira 2013, 47–50). Islamophobia, in contrast, is not a sharply defined phenomenon that can be scientifically measured. Rather, it is a combination of often subtle opinions and actions that occur within a range of intensity from passive acquiescence to articulate, committed belief in the stereotypes, and it has certainly created problems for Muslims.

There are few treatments of Muslims that portray them positively and realistically as full-dimensional and complex characters. One encounters, instead, a barrage of untruths and half-truths that seriously compromise the Muslim's collective personality, question behavior and motives, and undermine their role in society. These stereotypes suggest that all Muslims at least share some of the most common anti-societal and oppositional traits. Muslims are not given credit for being a people like any other—some good, some evil, some peaceful some violent—with a range of qualities and a variety of characteristics. Stereotyping does not do justice to the broad spectrum of Muslim identities and experiences. It assumes that there is a "Muslim" character, a "Muslim" personality and mind, in fact that we can speak of Islam as a monolithic faith and culture devoid of diversity, complexity, and regional and national differences. Islamophobic stereotyping fosters the false idea that there is no individual nature to Muslims—it creates a kind of abstract type, a figment of Western imagination, a caricatured "other" intent on doing harm to the values and social fabric of Western societies (Kundnani 2014; Esposito 1999; Kumar 2012).

Obviously, Islamophobia, even if it has some basis in rational fear, is harmful and dangerous because it has the potential to demonize all Muslims and Islam itself. But, as I have tried to argue, it is a prejudice of a different sort more akin to racism, sexism, ageism, and the like and cannot be compared to anti-Semitism that at its core is a form of Manichaeism, as Sartre labels it. Consider the term itself: a German anti-clerical racist, Wilhelm Marr, originally coined anti-Semitism in 1879 to put a modern face to an ancient hatred. Anti-Semitism as a modern movement purported to give a scientific basis to what it presented as opposition to some Jewish—or more precisely, "Semitic"—cultural, historical essence allegedly rooted in biology. Of course, the "scientific" basis of anti-Semitism was a completely absurd, distorted, and irrational claim. For Marr and his followers, anti-Semitism is not an attitude but an ideology. It is not intended as a description for a troubling social trend like Islamophobia but as the positive organizing principle of what anti-Semites see, ironically, as a progressive movement. Robert Wistrich in his epic study cited, as example, the French monarchist Charles Maurras' admiration for the intellectual simplicity of anti-Semitism, its ability to arrange, smooth over, and simplify the world. While the Jews and their allies appropriately regard anti-Semitism as propelled by hatred and irrational fear, anti-Semites regard themselves as a "movement" trying to improve the world. Rather than thinking of themselves as anti-moral and anti-humanitarian, the "moral" sensibility of anti-Semitism resides in its presentation of the Jews (or Jewishness, or Judaism) as a barrier to fair, open, and non-manipulated societies, to societies where the political, economic, and cultural "waters" can reach their natural levels, without interference. That is why anti-Semitism, unlike Islamophobia, is in essence an ideological phenomenon, even a spiritual one, and is not about likes and dislikes of character, a material battle over economic resources, or actual experiences with Jews.

Hearts and minds

This underscores one final distinction I would like to make. Unlike most other prejudices that do not foster intellectual traditions to support them, anti-Semitism has always had an ideational dimension—ancient, medieval, modern, and contemporary. It has been widely elaborated and encoded in texts, more so than other prejudices by far (Goldhagen 2013, 6–7). If hatred or phobias express themselves in discrimination and violence, anti-Semitism speaks and writes using words and concepts as well as actions. It has not been a mere reflex prejudice like most exclusionary prejudices including Islamophobia. Anti-Semitism has always been ideological and has produced vast literatures in many languages, across cultures, continents, and historical periods using virtually all forms of communication: written, oral, symbolic, and imagistic (Yakira 2013, 49–50). Compared to the more unarticulated forms of Islamophobia, which are typically vulgar, small-minded, ignorant, and occasionally violent, anti-Semitism has been an ideological phenomenon attractive to cultural elites. These "thinkers" have been against Jews or Judaism, Jewish habits of life and mind and, as argued throughout this paper, such a figment of fantastical imaginings and negative projections that they might as well have been describing a people that never existed.

Anti-Semitism is an enterprise of delegitimation—theologically, culturally, and politically. The logical conclusion of delegitimation is denying the group the right to exist, what Daniel Jonah Goldhagen labels eliminationist anti-Semitism and the Nazis called *Endlösung*, a final solution. Anti-Semitism has been a program for correcting, even saving, the world. This differentiates it from many other common prejudices which are primarily expressions of likes and dislikes that can certainly produce horrific oppression and discrimination, such as slavery or segregation, but do not portray a particular group as evil and in need of being destroyed (Goldhagen 2013, 36).

Implications

Because anti-Semites throughout the centuries have seen the problem of the Jews to be so acute and threatening, they produced anti-Semitic religious and secular ideologies and actions commensurate with the threat that Jews allegedly posed. These notions have included systematic discrimination, the establishment of ghettos, ethnic cleansing, the expulsion of Jews, riots, and pogroms leading ultimately to mass killings and genocide. Clearly, Islamophobia has not generated discrimination of such intensity and scope, but it certainly has done harm to Muslims through stereotyping and prejudice. On the ideological front, Islamophobia has the potential to mutate in the future to something akin to the potency of historic anti-Semitism. If the history of anti-Semitism teaches us anything, it is that an essentialist view of Judaism and Jews led to a phantom-like image of external danger with horrible consequences for Jews. I worry that the reified notions of Islam projecting the assumption that Muslims everywhere are the same and threatening, can eventually also lead to devastating effects. Islamist terrorism, violent protests against Danish cartoons, urban unrest in French suburbs, or young Muslims volunteering to join the jihadists are not explained in terms of specific social and political histories involved, but as symptoms of underlying conflict between Islam's cultural identity and Western values. This is dangerous since hatreds once unleashed are difficult if not impossible to contain. Anti-Semitism and Islamophobia, although different phenomena, do share one distinct characteristic: they are not strictly Jewish or Muslim problems. Yes, Jews and Muslims suffer, but we all are harmed and diminished by misconceptions and scapegoating left unattended.

Works Cited

Berman, Paul, 2003, Terror and Liberalism, New York: W.W. Norton and Company.

Esposito, John L., 1999, The Islamic Threat: Myth or Reality, New York: Oxford University Press.

Goldhagen, Daniel Jonah, 2013, The Devil That Never Dies: The Rise and Threat of Global Anti-Semitism, New York: Little, Brown and Company.

Harrison, Bernard, 2013, "Anti-Zionist, Anti-Semitism, and the Rhetorical Manipulation of Reality," in Alvin H. Rosenfeld, ed. Resurgent Anti-Semitism: Global Perspectives, Bloomington, IN: Indiana University Press, pp. 8–41.

Kumar, Deepa. 2012. Islamophobia and The Politics of Empire. New York: Haymarket Books.

Kundnani, Arun, 2014, The Muslims Are Coming!, London: Verso.

Mattson, Ingrid, 2011, "Address at the Sixty-ninth Conference of the General Assembly of the Union for Reform Judaism," in Reza Aslan, and Aaron J. Hahn Tapper, eds., Muslims and Jews in America, New York: Palgrave, pp. 127–132.

Nirenberg, David, 2013, Anti-Judaism: The Western Tradition, New York: W.W. Norton and Company.

Said, Edward, 1979, Orientalism, New York: Vintage.

Said, Edward, 1981, Covering Islam, New York: Pantheon.

Sartre, Jean-Paul, 1965, Anti-Semite and Jew, New York: Schoken Books.

Wistrich, Robert S., 2010, The Lethal Obsession: Anti-Semitism from Antiquity to the Global Jihad, New York: Random House.

Yakira, Elhanan, 2013, "Anti-Semitism and Anti-Zionism as a Moral Question," in Alvin H. Rosenfeld, ed., Resurgent Anti-Semitism: Global Perspectives, Bloomington, IN: Indiana University Press, pp. 42–64.

Yoffie, Rabbi Eric H., 2011, "Inaugural Address at the Forty-fourth Annual Convention of the Islamic Society of North America," in Reza Aslam, and Aaron J. Hahn Tapper, eds., Muslims and Jews in America, New York: Palgrave, pp. 121–125.

CROSSCURRENTS
CLASSIFYING MUSLIMS

Mohamed Mosaad Abdelaziz Mohamed

Since September 11, 2001, politicians, law enforcement, media, and academics have been trying to find the perfect classification of Muslims. The simplistic and unspoken but true question that lies in the heart of this classification is basically how we can distinguish the good Muslims from the bad Muslims. Equally important: Can we identify a set of markers that may help us predict a turn of a once a good Muslim into a terrorist? I will start this paper by exploring common classifications that have been proposed, propagated, and widely used in the West. Demonstrating the futility of these approaches, I will explain the epistemological principles on which Muslims classify themselves.

Western classification of Muslims

Several concepts have been used to describe "good" Islam—the kind of Islam that would create a good Muslim. Those concepts had, in fact, been used long before September 11, 2001. One must recall here concepts such as liberal, interpretive, modern, moderate, Sufi, and folk Islam. Liberal Islam, as presented by Charles Kurzman, has three tropes: liberal Šarī'ah, silent Šarī'ah, and interpreted Šarī'ah. On liberal Šarī'ah, Kurzman writes, "The liberal shari'a argues that the revelations of the Qur'an and the practices of the Prophet command Muslims to follow liberal positions" (Kurzman 1999, 11). The world religion of Islam that emerged more than 14 centuries ago is supposed to match "liberal positions." By silent Šarī'ah, Kurzman refers to the argument "that the shari'a is silent on certain topics—not because divine revelation was incomplete or faulty, but because the revelation intentionally left certain issues for humans to choose" (12). Šarīʿah, in this sense, seems more like a set of limited legal injunctions rather than rules, principles, traditions, debates, objectives, and discursive articulations of historical realities. Finally, interpreted Šarīʿah, another supposedly desirable character, is akin to what I call interpretive Islam.

Interpretive Islam is perceived as an opposite to literalist Islam, a classification that emerged probably from the problems of Christian history in the West. The opposition hardly speaks to the reality of Muslims, for Islamic scripture has always been subject to interpretations. Except for the marginal Ẓāhirī School in Islamic law, one can find a variety of schools that have had different approaches and methods of interpreting the Qurʾān and Ḥadīth. A more subtle definition of interpretive Islam was proposed by a number of modern Muslim intellectuals, such as Arkun, Hanafi, Soroush, and Abu Zayd. Here, scripture is articulated as a historical and human piece of literature. Those intellectuals do not necessarily deny a metaphysical dimension of scripture, but they insist that this dimension is not accessible to the human labor of interpretation. Humans can only treat scripture objectively and rationally as literature. Saba Mahmood offered an excellent critique of these approaches, which she called secular hermeneutics: "Underlying this hermeneutical project is a secularized conception of religion in which religion is understood to be an abstracted category of beliefs and doctrines from which the individual believer stands apart to examine, compare and evaluate its various manifestations" (Mahmood 2006, 341).

Since the nineteenth century, Western scholars have questioned Islam's compatibility with modernity. Surveying Western articulation of this question, Armando Salvatore and Muhammad Masud wrote:

> Western scholars were nevertheless divided on the question whether Muslim societies can be modernized. One group maintained that "Islam is in its very nature incapable of reform and progressive adaptation to the expansion of human knowledge" (Stoddard 1921, 33). In their view, Muslim societies could not survive in the process of global change. Others believed that Muslim societies have no choice but to modernize. However, they could do so only by adopting to the Western model. (Masud and Salvatore 2009, 39–40)

Accordingly, we seem to have two essentialized forms, that of "modernity" and of "Islam," and they are deemed incompatible.

The term "moderate Islam" might be the most confusing term reference to good Islam. Muqtedar Khan writes that moderate Muslims "argue that Islam embodies a message of compassion and peace sent by God to civilize humanity and to give human existence a transcendent and divine purpose. They are aghast at—and reject—the use of Islam to incite terror, justify bigotry, and discriminate on the basis of faith, gender, or ethnicity" (Khan 2003, 418). The definition is not helpful because of its enormous flexibility. It is flexible enough that the government of the United States has recently announced its plans to arm the *moderate* rebels, who fight a civil war against the political regime of the Syrian state.

Two other kinds of supposedly good and desirable Islam seem to be Sufi Islam and folk Islam. Usually, they are seen in opposition to textual Islam. Sufi Islam is proposed as a spiritual—that is apolitical—form of Islam, which propagates values such as love, tolerance, and unity (see Schwartz 2008). Folk Islam, on the other hand, is supposedly a popular form of Islam that is tolerant in attitude and syncretic in formation. Joyce Fleuckiger called it vernacular Islam. She wrote: "*In Amma's Healing Room* is a study of particular expressions of vernacular Islam that reveal to us the potential flexibility and creativity of Islam, a tradition that is often viewed by both Muslims and non-Muslims alike to be universal, singular and monolithic" (Fleuckiger 2006, xii).

The above classifications have serious problems that made them persistently useless. Liberal Islam presupposes a historical, socio-political, and secular ideology to define what Islam, as a world religion, is. This approach strikes down any claim of authenticity and makes it the least appealing form of Islam to be adopted by Muslims. Silent Šarī'ah, proposed by Kurzman as a modern approach to Islam, has been a normative approach in *uṣūlī* literature,[1] usually discussed under *Istisḥāb*.[2] There is an interesting discussion of it in Yūsuf al-Qaraḍāwī's book, *'Awāmil al-Si'ah wa al-Murūnah fī al-Šarī'ah al-Islāmiyyah* (2002, 15).

The historicity of scripture, which is the proposal of advocates of interpretive Šarī'ah, has persistently been an integral part of traditional approaches by Muslim scholars. In addition to the numerous classic works that have articulated the linguistic aspects of scripture, Muslim scholars have agreed that the meaning of scriptural words can be found in the use of these words by Arabs who lived during the age of revelation. Moreover, to reveal the meaning of a Qur'ānic verse or a report of Ḥadīth, one must consult two genres in Islamic knowledge, known as *asbāb al-nuzūl* and *asbāb al-wurūd*. These two genres discuss the historical situation (in which a particular verse or report was revealed) as a necessary piece of knowledge to understand its meaning. The only difference in the proposed approach of interpretive Šarī'ah, therefore, is its being secular—the insistence on isolating the metaphysical dimension from the text.

When modern Islam is introduced in opposition to traditional Islam, tradition is defined as essentially stagnant and foreign to the present time. Given the supposed rupture between tradition and modernity, Muslims must recreate new forms of religion to fit in the new reality. This ideological proposition ignores a more subtle historical and ethnographic understanding of tradition as an ongoing process that constantly includes both continuity and change.

Finally, let us have a word about vernacular Islam. In his important article, "The Idea of an Anthropology of Islam," Talal Asad refutes the notion that Islam is what Muslim informants claim it to be:

> There are everywhere Muslims who say that what *other* people take to be Islam is not really Islam at all. This paradox cannot be resolved simply by saying that the claim as to what is Islam will be admitted by the anthropologist only where it applies to the informant's *own* beliefs and practices, because it is generally impossible to define beliefs and practices in terms of an isolated subject. (Asad 2009, 3)

Asad also rejects the dichotomy of folk Islam versus scripturalist Islam, a notion popularized by Ernest Gellner and Clifford Geertz. He argues that "it is wrong to represent types of Islam as being correlated with types of social structures" (Asad 2003, 10), such as urban or rural.

> If one wants to write an anthropology of Islam, one should begin, *as Muslims do*, from the concept of a discursive tradition that includes and relates itself to the founding texts of the Qur'an and the Hadith. Islam is neither a distinctive social structure, nor heterogeneous collection of beliefs, artifacts, customs, and morals. It is a tradition. (Asad 2003, 20; emphasis added)

The problem with the concept of a moderate Islam is that moderation is culturally and subjectively defined. It is simply too ambiguous to be useful. Sufi Islam, too, is quite problematic. In his classic, *Realm of the Saint*, Vincent Cornell argues that "apart from holy warriors and tribal eponyms, the most important saints of early Moroccan Sufism were legal specialists" (Cornell 1998, 7). Creating a classification, where Sufis are opposed to scripturalists and legal specialists, is simply false. In addition, correlating Sufism with peace ignores the history of Sufism, where Sufis were actively engaged in *jihād*, and their masters were praised for their fighting skills and brevity in wars.

From a practical point of view, the above terms are not helpful. If we assume modern Islam to be such a good phenomenon, will we also accept political Islam, since it too is a modern form of Islam? Salafī Islam is used as a form of supposedly bad traditional, non-modern Islam. Christopher Blanchard (2007) in a report for the American Congress (con)fuses Salafī Islam with Wahhābī Islam and argues that they are the root of terrorism. In sharp contrast to Blanchard's report, Spalek and Robert (2008) argue that Salafī Muslims can and should be engaged in counter-terrorism work with the police. Although literalist approaches to Qur'ān and Ḥadīth are routinely condemned as promoting violence, the opposite might be more accurate: Indeed, literalist Wahhābī scholars are prohibiting suicide bombing, since suicide is not permitted in scripture. There are, on the other hand, Hamas scholars among others who allow these operations through a rational interpretive reading that favors realistic and historical conditions over the letter of the law.

Muslim classification of Muslims

In *The Archaeology of Knowledge*, Foucault explains how the power of discourse hides in classifications, specifically in what he calls *points of diffraction*. These are points of incompatibility: two contradictory concepts or objects. Those contradictory elements are formed on the same basis and by the same rules, and hence are also characterized as *points of equivalence*. Instead of constituting a mere defect of coherence, they appear as alternatives in the form of 'either ... or'. Lastly, they are characterized as *link points of systematization*. On the basis of each of these equivalent elements is derived a coherent series of objects, concepts, and statements with new possible points of incompatibility within each of them (Foucault 1972,

65–66). Classifications, such as liberal and conservative, interpretive and literalist, or vernacular and scripturalist are power-loaded formations.

Equally important here are the conditions of emergence of discourses. Discourses emerge in a context of other discourses, with which they share *rules of formation* and a *system of dispersion*. Foucault explains the *authorities of delimitation* as well. To examine a Western discourse of Islam, therefore, we must situate it in its Western, secular, and Christian contexts.

Here, then, I want to focus only on two points that affect our academic approaches to Islam. First, I will examine the treatment of Islam as an ideological and moral tradition to argue that *form* is more important than *content* in Muslims' classification of themselves. Second, I will analyze the introduction of different versions of Islam that are defined as specific choices in order to argue that a no-choice attitude, driven by logic of the dual, has been the norm in Islamic formations. Finally, I will provide brief reflections on the possibility of predicting terrorism.

The priority of form

In his famous critique of Geertz's definition of religion, Talal Asad rejects the possibility of having a universal definition of religion, "because that definition is itself the historical product of discursive processes" (Asad 1993, 29). Among other things, Asad criticizes Geertz's emphasis on belief. "Geertz's treatment of religious belief," he writes, "which lies at the core of his conception of religion, is a modern, privatized Christian one because and to the extent that it emphasizes the priority of belief as a state of mind rather than as constituting activity in the world" (47). Asad situates this conceptualization of religion within the formations of the modern state. "The suggestion that religion has a universal function in belief is one indication of how marginal religion has become in modern industrial society as the site for producing disciplined knowledge and personal discipline" (46). The notion of "personal discipline" brings us right to Foucault's *The History of Sexuality*.

Foucault recognizes two different forms of morality, which he calls *codes of behavior* and *forms of subjectivation*. Though these two forms are not entirely dissociated, they may develop in relative independence. In different moralities, the emphasis may be put on one or the other. In Greek and Greco-Roman antiquity, according to Foucault, the focus is on subjectivation. That is also the case in Christianity. By subjectivation, Foucault refers to a conscious relationship with the self, where the ethical subject deliberately transforms himself. This process "requires him to act upon himself, to monitor, test, improve, and transform himself. … In these conditions, the contradictory movements of the soul—much more than the carrying out of the acts themselves—will be the prime material of moral practice" (Foucault 1990, 28, 26).

It is this focus on belief as a state of mind and a morality that proceeds from consciousness that the project of self-creation emerges. It is a moral transformation that produces a disciplined, controlled, and beautiful self. Through these moral and rational mechanisms of subjectivation—where meaning is central—private, individual, functional, re-formed, rationalized, disciplined, liberal, moderate, and modern Muslims are supposed to be created. All these processes and formations, however, are not central in the history of Islam.

Islam, a Semitic and legal tradition, shifts the emphasis away from ideology—that is away from theology and morality—as subjectivation toward the formalities of the law and the empty structures of ritual.[3] The Qur'ān says, "Do not let the hatred of a people prevent you from being just. Be just; that is nearer to righteousness" (Noble Qur'ān, Sūrah 5: Āyah 8). It ignores bad feelings, such as hatred, and stresses a practical point: be just! Thoughts, bad thoughts included, do not matter as long as they do not transform into action in the world. In another striking example, the Qur'ān says, "And if two factions among the believers should fight, then make settlement between the two" (Noble Qur'ān, Sūrah 49: Āyah 9). Here, the verse attends neither to their motives nor to their ideology. In fact, it considers both of them "believers."

In the formation of Islam, the emphasis moves away from notions such as meaning or truth in favor of obedience. What matters the most is the collective practice of ritual and the inter-subjective observance of the law, but not the transformation of the self or of individual ideology. Morality comes as codes of behavior, in the Foucauldian sense. Foucault writes that in this kind of morality, the focus is on "the instances of authority that enforce the code, that require it to be learned and observed, that penalize infractions; in these conditions, the subjectivation occurs basically in a quasi-juridical form, where the ethical subject refers his conduct to a law, or set of laws" (Foucault 1972, 29). In other words, unlike in liberal, modern, and moderate Islams, where the emphasis is on ideology and the transformation of the self—that is, on *content*—in traditional Islam the emphasis is on method—that is, on *form*.

Muslims classify themselves according to juridical schools. Differences among these schools are differences of formal methods. Discussions and disputes are mainly legal. They are conducted through comparing methods and debating the technical accuracy of their use. Choices of war and peace are not legitimized by ideologies or subjective moralities. They are legal decisions based on the application of the forms of legal methods. To give just one example, the Wahhābī jurist, who prohibited suicide bombing, would quite comfortably sentence to death an adulterous married man or woman by stoning. Again, what is consistent in these seemingly contradictory rulings is not the content, say, the protection or disregard of life. Rather, it is the formal method.

The dual

Divinity in Islam is neither incarnated nor hiding in history or protruding from underneath the surface in the history of Islam's chosen people. Divinity in Islam is *almost* withdrawing. With no dramatic entry into history in terms of miracles, the Qur'ān remains for Muslims the only contingent relationship with the Divine. This historical absence of truth creates *reversibility*. In *Reification*, Timothy Bewes explores this reversibility of concepts. He roots it in the ambiguity of the impossibly reifiable that is reified out of linguistic necessity.

> Reversibility implies a certain underlying assumption: that there is an other to language, something completely outside the text and inarticulable by it; that the text is as nothing, merely thinglike, in relation to this outside; and that to speak in the name of this inarticulable otherness is necessarily to elaborate, or simply to presuppose the contradictory aspect of everything that constitutes the here and now. (Bewes 2002, 202, 3)

Language, therefore, is an impossible host for truth. The direct consequence of this semiotic reality is a situation that favors a no-choice attitude, an attitude that has characterized the history of Sunni Islam: The Qur'ān is neither absolutely divine nor completely historical; God's attributes are to be understood neither literally nor metaphorically; freedom of choice is neither absolutely granted nor completely restricted by God's destiny, etc. In place of a dialectic reason, where thesis and antithesis negate each other to produce a new thesis, which will eventually undergo the same fate (since this process unfolds perpetually through history), what we find in historical formations of Islam is the *logic of the dual*, where speakers neither choose between two opposing theses nor integrate them. Rather, they find ambiguous paths in between them.

Exploring theological schools in Islam, one finds an interesting phenomenon. All opinions and groups that made a clear choice were immediately rejected and turned into marginal sects. Mainstream Sunni Islam is made of major schools, which preserved a characteristically swinging dynamism of discourse. The conscious avoidance of making a final articulation of "truth" produced two important phenomena: First, it located meaning not in reason but in the collective performance of ritual—and hence the emphasis on *form*. Second, it produced classifications not as logical opposites but as reversible duals.

To give one more example, I will go back to the legal schools. Even the clear emphasis on form and obedience operates with the "dual" in relation to *maṣlaḥah*, or public interest. Public interest is a rational concept that is in a constant dual relationship with the letter of the text. A jurist typically swings back and forth between these two formations when articulating his or her historical ruling. To find *maṣlaḥah* inside scripture, one must raise the question of reason. Why is scripture introducing this or that injunction? The reason of an injunction is called *ḥikmah*. Nevertheless, *uṣūlī* scholars replaced this word with another word: *'illah*. *'Illah*, too, means reason. However, conceptually, *'illah* in fact destabilizes reason as the ground of any injunction. For instance, a report of Ḥadīth will recommend that a traveler should not be fasting. The logical reason of this dispensation—that is *ḥikmah*—is hardship. But scholars will typically use *'illah*, and in this case, the *'illah* is the traveling itself. Even if a Muslim has only a very brief flight, he or she may not fast. Hardship, the *ḥikmah*, does not matter. What matters is traveling itself, an act that is measured by distance, not use of energy.

In light of the *logic of the dual*, examining Western classifications of Islam, such as interpretive, vernacular, or Sufi, will reveal their serious fault. All of these concepts are proposed as definite choices: reading scripture as historical literature, *not* a metaphysical one; practicing Islam as a cultural tradition, *not* a scripturalist one; struggling to have ecstatic unity with God through spiritual and ascetic forms of practice, *not* legal or ritual ones, etc. Sunni Muslims do not make definite choices. For instance, the historicity of scripture has always been a part of every reading of scripture in Islam. Scholars have agreed that there are text passages that must be read as historical pieces because they are bound to their specific historical reality. Other pieces must be read as eternal. Scholars have, however, never agreed upon which pieces belong to this or that division. Uṣūlī scholars have included ʿurf (customs of local people) as one of the non-textual sources of legislation. Vernacular Islam, in this sense, is a legitimate part of Šarīʿah. It is legitimate, however, as long as it is harmonious with other parts of the law. Or, to name another example, elements and practices of Sufism have been widely adopted by jurists. Ibn ʿAṭāʾ Allāh al-Sakandarī (1260–1309 CE), for instance, was both a Mālikī jurist and a Sufi teacher who taught at al-Azhar Mosque.

Prediction

Don Handelman (2013) used Deleuze and Guattari's metaphor of the *rhizome* to explain the qualities of asymmetry, speed, intensity, laterality, and penetration used by terrorist organizations. I propose using this metaphor not only to understand modes of organization, but also to comprehend modes of identity and being. Deleuze and Guattari contrast the tree, a rational model of classification, to the desire-driven rhizome. They write: "Principles of connection and heterogeneity: any point of a rhizome can be connected to anything other, and must be. This is very different from the tree or root, which plots a point, fixes an order" (Deleuze and Guattari 1987, 7).

Religiously moderates, such as Hamas members, can be politically radical. Traditionalists can be apolitical, such as Salafī Muslims (like most of the Saudi Wahhābīs), Jihādis (like al-Qāʿidah group members), or Sufis (like the popular preacher ʿAlī al-Jafrī). An Egyptian Muslim Brotherhood member can be either Salafī and rationalist, or rationalist and liberal. Assigning specific ideologies to specific groups and individuals is a futile project. Islamic identities are like literature that is "an assemblage." "It has nothing to do with ideology. There is no ideology and never has been. All we talk about are multiplicities, lines, strata and segmentaries, lines of flight and intensities, machinic assemblages and their various types ..." (Deleuze and Guattari 1987, 4). This is not to say classifications are impossible. It is only to say that to try to classify Muslims according to rational tree classifications is an illusion.

Notes

1. The literature that discusses the principles of law.
2. It is the belief that the past or present matter must be assumed to remain as it is in the present or future.
3. I am using *ritual* here, as it is used in Habermas and Baudrillard, even though neither of them use this concept to refer to modern societies. In Habermas, archaic societies are integrated through the practice of ritual without strictly having any cognitive content. It is a state of social integration in which language has only minimal significance (Habermas 1987, 9). Baudrillard proposes *rituality* as opposed to modern sociality. Central to his world of rituality is the game, which is played with rules not laws. Unlike laws, rules rule by obligation, not enforcement, and they have no psychological, metaphysical, or rational foundation. Passion, appearance, play, and destiny are what he attributes to rituality, the game, and its rules. In the game, one escapes meaning (Baudrillard 1990, 131, 132).

Works Cited

Al-Qaraḍāwī, Yūsuf, 2002, ʿAwāmil al-Siʿah wa al-Murūnah fī al-Šarīʿah al-Islāmiyyah, Kuwait: al-Majlis al-Waṭanī lil-Thaqāfah wa al-Funūn wa al-Ādāb.

Asad, Talal, 1993, Genealogies of Religion: Discipline and Reasons of Power in Christianity and Islam, Baltimore: The Johns Hopkins University Press.

Asad, Talal, 2003, Formations of the Secular: Christianity, Islam, Modernity, California: Stanford University Press.

Asad, Talal, 2009, "The Idea of an Anthropology of Islam," Qui Parle **17/2** (Spring/Summer), pp. 1–30.

Baudrillard, Jean, 1990, Seduction, New York: St. Martin's Press, 1990.

Bewes, Timothy, 2002, Reification or the Anxiety of Late Capitalism, New York: Verso, 2002.

Blanchard, Christopher M., 2007, "The Islamic Traditions of Wahhabism and Salafiyya," Congressional Research Service **RS21432** (January), pp. 1–6.

Cornell, Vincent J., 1998, Realm of the Saint: Power and Authority in Moroccan Sufism, Austin: University of Texas Press.

Deleuze, Gilles, and Félix Guattari, 1987, A Thousand Plateaus: Capitalism and Schizophrenia, Minneapolis: University of Minnesota Press.

Fleuckiger, Joyce, 2006, In Amma's Healing Room: Gender and Vernacular Islam in South India, Bloomington: Indiana University Press.

Foucault, Michel, 1972, The Archaeology of Knowledge and the Discourse of Language, New York: Pantheon Books.

Foucault, Michel, 1990, The History of Sexuality: The Use of Pleasure, New York: Vintage Books.

Habermas, Jürgen, 1987, The Theory of Communicative Action, Volume Two: Lifeworld and System: A Critique of Functionalist Reason, Boston: Beacon Press, 1987.

Handelman, Don, 2013, "Self-Exploders, Self-Sacrifice, and the Rhizomic Organization of Terrorism," in Galina Lindquist, and Don Handelman, eds., Religion, Politics and Globalization: Anthropological Approaches, New York: Berghahn Books, pp. 231–62.

Khan, Muqtedar, 2003, "Radical Islam, Liberal Islam," Current History **102**(668), pp. 417–21.

Kurzman, Charles, 1999, "Liberal Islam: Prospects and Challenges," Middle East Review of International Affairs **3/3** (September), pp. 11–9.

Mahmood, Saba, 2006, "Secularism, Hermeneutics, and Empire: The Politics of Islamic Reformation," Public Culture **18**(2), pp. 323–47.

Masud, Muhammad Khalid, and Armando Salvatore, 2009, "Western Scholars of Islam on the Issue of Modernity," in M. K. Masud, A. Salvatore, and van Bruinessen Martin, eds., Islam and Modernity: Key Issues and Debates, Cairo: The American University in Cairo Press, pp. 39–40.

Schwartz, Stephen, 2008, The Other Islam: Sufism and the Road to Global Harmony, New York: Doubleday.

Spalek, Basia, and Lambert Robert, 2008, "Muslim Communities, Counter-Terrorism and Counter-Radicalisation: A Critically Reflective Approach to Engagement," International Journal of Law, Crime and Justice **36**, pp. 257–70.

CROSSCURRENTS

NOSTALGIA AND MEMORY IN JEWISH–MUSLIM ENCOUNTERS

Mehnaz M. Afridi

Anti-Semitism and Islamophobia have sparked recent and major discussions in the media and academic circles. Sometimes, the two racial terms are seen alongside one another, and at other times, they are seen on different trajectories and paths. I argue that these prejudices are connected by a variegated history and memory.

> Our new identity proclaimed openly our opposition to Israel and Zionism—and proclaimed implicitly our opposition to the "Zionists" in our midst, Egyptian Jews. For although explicitly Zionism was distinguished from Jewishness, an undercurrent meaning "Jewish" was also contained in the word. The word "Arab," emerging at this moment to define our identity, silently carried within it its polar opposite—Zionist/Jew—without which hidden, silent connotation it actually had no meaning. For the whole purpose of its emergence now was precisely to tell us of our new alignments and realignments in relation to both terms, Arab and Jew. (Ahmed 2000, 246)

> For as long as I can remember, I remember fear. Existential fear. The Israel I grew up in—the Israel of the mid-1960s—was energetic, exuberant, and hopeful.... One day, I dreaded that the dark ocean would rise and drown us all. A mythological tsunami would strike our shores and sweep my Israel away. It would become another Atlantis, lost in the depths of the sea. (Shavit 2013, i)

Contemporaries like Leila Ahmed, an Egyptian Muslim woman, and Ari Shavit, an Israeli man, point out that fear, memory, and realignments of both Jewish and Arab identities were transformed in the 1960s. Today, once again, this theme recurs in the public arena of Jewish–Muslim relations. The events in Paris in January 2015 compel us to reflect on several violent acts in France, including the 2006 kidnapping, torture, and murder of Ilan Halimi by the so-called Gang des Barbares, the slaughter of children at a Jewish day school by Mohammed Merah in 2012, and the carnage unleashed at the Jewish Museum of Brussels by French national Mehdi Nemmouche. The attack against the French satirical magazine *Charlie Hebdo* created an uproar. During the shooting in the Paris kosher grocery store, *Hyper Cacher,* ironically, it was a Muslim employee, Lassana Bathily, who saved Jews by hiding them in a walk-in freezer. He is quoted as saying, "We are brothers. It's not a question of Jews, of Christians, or of Muslims. We're all in the same boat; we have to help each other to get out of this crisis."[1] The responses to these acts have, so far, been marked by sorrow, regret, and confusion. How can we comprehend the rampage and mistrust between the Jewish and Muslim communities? Currently, there is no compelling analysis to explain how and why Muslims and Jews in France are experiencing a rise of anti-Semitism and Islamophobia from either extremist "Muslim" groups or right-wing domestic groups.

Such acts of violence under the guise of faith, as well as acts of kindness in the face of such violence, demonstrate a need for revision, reform, and de-colonization of many parts of the colonized Muslim world. The so-called clash of East and West, or civilized and uncivilized worlds, seems to have been reignited. This clash is not simply a binary struggle against a homogenized religion or culture. Rather, it relates to complex and nuanced identities that are challenged by the history of Islam, colonialism, wars, genocide, and internal conflicts.

Muslims are facing many global issues, some dating back to the crusades, colonialism, and communism, while others are connected to genocide, imperialism, and the 9/11 attack. With the recent outbreaks of anti-Semitism and Islamophobia, especially in Europe, we have moved to another phase of extremism. More than just memories, we can speak of consecrated "traces"[2] that are dividing us and others.

Debates on the nature and proper role of Islam are, of course, steeped in a sense of the past, in memories of what Islam has been and how it has operated in society over the last fourteen centuries. These memories are not mere shadows: They shape discussion and conflict in very direct ways. It is memory that identifies goals and purposes within the religious-secular-extremist debate (Humphreys 1999). No group in contemporary Islam would dare to create something new. Rather, each group claims—and surely believes—that it is trying to recapture the essence of pure Islam that once existed.

Our memory of what has been Islam[3] is related to our ability to gain an understanding of human reality and recapture the essence of something that has been lost. The same can be said, of course, of Judaism. How do Jews and Muslims remember their traditions and their relations with each other in light of their respective traditions? How does this paradox shape contemporary Jewish–Muslim relations?

I suggest that Jews and Muslims today remember each other's faith and historical identity through a radically different lens. The nostalgia that Islam and Judaism have constructed through a theological, historical, and political lens is, one could argue, the central issue of Jewish–Muslim tensions. There have been, for example, numerous discussions on fear: psychological fear, cultural fear, and the memory of fear regarding the loss of religious identity. Religious conflicts, violence, and terror are currently debated in the academic and socio-political arena. William T. Cavanaugh's *The Myth of Religious Violence: Secular Ideology and the Roots of Modern Conflict* (2009), for example, draws on significant factors that are crucial in the perceptions of other religions and genocides. The views regarding the religion of the other are, for the most part, imaginary, creating fear of the other. Memories that Jews and Muslims have of one another highlight the underlying, crucial problem in their modern-day perception of each other. Whether Jews are viewed as colonizers or Muslims as extremists, these stark images draw on the vulnerability of each religion.

The religion of the other is perceived as violent, creating falsifying myths and mistrust. Juergensmeyer contends, "Religion seems to be connected with violence virtually everywhere" (cited in Cavanaugh 2009, 28). This, Juergensmeyer claims, is true across all religious traditions and has always been so. He does not consider it to be an aberration. "Rather, I look for explanations in the current forces of geopolitics and in a strain of violence that may be found at the deepest levels of the religious imagination" (cited in Cavanaugh 2009, 28). Cavanaugh's book is important to the study of religion and the depiction of other religions. Referring to Juergensmeyer's work, he states: "More specifically, religious images of struggle and transformation—'cosmic war'—have a tendency to foster violence when transferred to 'real-world' conflicts by 'satanizing' the other and ruling out compromise or peaceful existence" (Cavanaugh 2009, 28–29). Religious wars maintain a transfixed memory that creates fear and leads to the dehumanization of the other. The images embedded in memory retain the crucial binary between groups that foster a radical division and question how one can remember a tradition and, simultaneously, reimagine a tradition. "Humiliated memory thus forces us into an unnatural relation with the past, because the knowledge it imparts crushes the spirit and frustrates the incentive to renewal" (Langer 1991, 79).

How do we remember our traditions without a longing for resuscitation or purification? What do we remember? And who in our memory is the "other"? Bernard Lewis's "Roots of Muslim Rage" (1990)[4] and Samuel Huntington's "Clash of Civilizations" (1993)[5] began a controversial discussion about a future crisis that would be based on differences in culture, religion, and identity. However, divisions have existed since the advent of Islam, when Muslims first encountered Jews. Memory perception considers the early Muslim and Jewish interaction in Medina as hostile and, sometimes, genocidal. This particular perception clearly highlights the way in which our memory of one another has come to bear upon our psyche. Memories of religious tension go back 1400 years and have become the specter of today's mistrust and violence. Sadly, the cooperation that once existed between these traditions has been lost over time.

> The most ubiquitous comparison relates anti-Semitism to discrimination against today's Muslims on a qualitative basis. A better understanding of these fundamental differences can be achieved through studies that analyze the forms and tropes of images of Jews and Muslims. In particular, a study from Spain by Baer and Lopez is quite revealing. They found images portraying Jews as "ultra-modern: intelligent, rational, business-oriented," while images of Muslims implied that they were "still in the Middle Ages: religious, backwards, sexist." The imaginary Jew is perceived as being the incarnation of the value of modern mercantile world and is thought to govern the world behind the scenes, whereas an

imaginary Arab [is perceived as] a noble savage uncontaminated by the spirit of modern economics. (Jikeli 2015, 30–31)

Considering the framework of these negative images of Jews and Muslims in their current forms in Europe, several questions arise: Can a lens that remains arrested in the past of one's own tradition ever give license to a quest for peace? Furthermore, can the longstanding perceptions of the respective other tradition allow the quest for peace between these groups to achieve success?

Early Jewish–Muslim interactions

As we experience Islamophobia and anti-Semitism globally today, it is important to analyze the multiple trajectories of Jewish–Muslim interactions from the beginning of Islam, including Qur'anic injunctions against Jews and others, as well as the Jewish recorded memory of Muslims and their encounter with them. Memories of one another began in Arabia in the seventh century, when the new believers of an emerging Islam established their own particular message and view of the world. The Qur'an and the Hadith mention that the Prophet Muhammad (*Peace be upon him*) and his followers came into contact with Jews. "This particular contact became extremely important because reactions to it were recorded for posterity in the Qur'an. The only sources for the earliest relations between Jews and Muslims are the Qur'an and its attendant literatures, which, like other sacred literatures, are interested in history only insofar as it helps to define the emerging community and its values and ideas."[6]

Focusing on exclusivist verses or particular verses that are quoted by extremist groups has, however, created a division among Muslims and others. This is evident in the case of certain Medinian Jews: Despite their relative proximity to Muslims theologically, some sections of the Qur'an's harshly criticize—doctrinally or otherwise—these individuals. By the same token, the Qur'an refers to other Jews who may be saved (Surah 2:62 and 5:69; see also Khalil 2012, 138).[7]

The encounter between Jews and Muslims in Medina has been discussed throughout the years by Jewish and Muslim scholars and theologians. However, interest in these early encounters recorded in the Qur'an has been revived in a contemporary light; thus, the encounters play a significant role in the people's conceptions of the early Jewish–Muslim communities. The sense of fear, abandonment, and mistrust—one might dare referring here to a mechanism of *victimizing one another*—is being established through sacred narratives that have been brought to light in contemporary political situations of anti-Semitism and Islamophobia.

The Jewish memory of early Muslims is full of terror and fear, while the Muslim encounter recorded in the Qur'an is full of mistrust. Many examples exemplify how Jews were perceived by Muslims and illustrate that this memory perception is still alive. For instance, in his book, *European Muslim Antisemitism: Why Young Urban Males Say They Don't Like Jews* (2015), Gunther Jikeli refers to a survey he conducted that demonstrates how prevalent the memory of a struggle and conflict remains in the minds of young urban Muslim males. Images that blame Jews as having created trouble for Muslims are a common theme with no historical or religious evidence. Jikeli notes:

> Participants often referred to "Islamic history" or conflicts between Muhammad and his adherents, on one side, and Jewish tribes, on the other, to illustrate and justify enmity against Jews for things "they" did in the past or part of an ongoing historical struggle with the Jews. However, references to Islamic history were usually vague. The following French interviewee's argument is a good example. He was not sure what particular kind of mischief Jews made, but he was adamant that "the Jews" are to blame, that what they did was unforgivable, and that their actions resulted in eternal animosity between Muslims and Jews.

Sabri We have a history with them [...], I don't know that much about this kind of thing, but a long time ago, I think they were the ones who betrayed the prophet [...]. After that, the Muslims, there's a story like that. Yeah, that's one thing, it's something that makes it worth going to war with them.

Interviewer Even now?

Sabri No, not war, but to...well, we don't talk to them [...] It's not war between the Arabs and the Jews, I don't know...it's about religion [...]. They did something that wasn't good, and it's unpardonable [...]. It's weird you can't, everyone is obsessed about it [...]. They have to change. It's the Jews who did something bad [...]. It's too late. It was at the beginning, [and] given the way they are. (Jikeli 2015, 135–6)

The story of the first encounters between Jews and Muslims seems to have created a negative memory for both Jews and Muslims. In Medina, when Islam was just gaining power, Muslims encountered Jews who did not accept Islam or Mohammed (*Peace be upon him*) as their prophet and messenger (which was also true of Christians).

All negative descriptions of Jews recorded in the Qur'an and early Islamic literature (Hadith) were a result of the friction between the early Muslim community and the organized Jewish communities (tribes) of Medina. The Qur'an represents itself as a universal teaching; hence, its rhetorical style appears to refer negatively to Jews in general terms. Since for Muslim believers the Qur'an is inimitable scripture (the inimitability of the Qur'an is an absolute dogma of Islamic theology), the negative portrayal of Jews represents a level of truth that is extremely difficult to question. As scripture, the Qur'an is a powerful foundation for the worldview of Muslims around the globe. The kind of intercommunal conflicts we witness today may be only a few years old, but the verses of scripture have an eternal quality to them.[8]

The foundation for the worldviews of contemporary Muslims becomes highly problematic in light of the anti-Semitism that Jews are experiencing from Muslims, either through propaganda or through violence. The Jewish response to the early encounter with Muslims was based on the belief that they were massacred at the hands of early Muslims. "From the Jewish side, the response toward Islam could take the form of revolt (*Isawiyya*), rejection (polemics) debate (in salons, homes, and marketplaces), or conversion (Abdallah Ibn Salam)" (Wasserstrom 1995, 11). At that time, Jews feared the erection of a new authoritative religion that could threaten them. To mention one example: "Jews of the Qurayza surrendered. Trenches were dug in the marketplace of Medina, Jews were brought out in batches, and per Muhammad's order, they were struck in those trenches. Sources estimate the number of people killed that day to range from 600 to 900" (Firestone 2008, 38). This account, in the memory of Jews, is seen as the first massacre under early Islam.

The negative memory of warring Muslims is further exacerbated by the image of the Ishmaelites, as Muslims were referred to by Jews.

Although Islam is linked to the genealogy of Abraham through the Torah, it is Isaac who is considered to be the true heir of Abraham, while the descendants of Abraham's other son, Ishmael, are depicted as nomadic hunters who inhabited a wide swath of the Middle East. Through this association, later texts connected Islam to the negative image of Ishmael in the Torah. Ishmael, as the negative counterpart of Isaac, is associated with the unrighteous descendants of Abraham, while the descendants of Isaac are seen as God's chosen people. In the book of Job, the Ishmaelites are portrayed as thieves: "The tents of the robbers prosper, and they that provoke God are secure since God brought them with His hand" (Job 12); in later Rabbinical writings, Ishmael is depicted as having violated the three cardinal sins of idolatry, sexual immorality, and murder (Genesis Rabah 53, PT Sotah 6:6; see Brill 2012, 146).

These very early perceptions of Muslims and Jews find themselves enveloped in the politics of today's extremist Muslim groups, like ISIS and al-Qaeda. They are also found in the rhetoric of Jews who believe that, like the Ishmaelites, Muslims are violent and aggressive. The two opposing images, formed in the imagination and memory of Jews and Muslims, foil any understanding of historical context. This hindrance has become even more pronounced in light of the advent of the state of Israel, the war between Israelis and Palestinians, and the image of all Jews as Zionists, as previously illustrated by Leila Ahmed. Although Ahmed is referring to Arabs, not Muslims, the memory of the moment that she describes takes place in all Muslim countries, regardless of ethnicity, since Muslims consider themselves to exist under the umbrella of Islam as the *ummah* (community). Jews, on the other hand, live with Shavit's existential fear: it is a fear of losing an identity that is rooted securely in a Jewish land. Indeed, this fear has been enflamed by rabbinic images of Ishmael and the massacre of Jews in the trenches of Medina.

The early encounter of Jews and Muslims is but one example of how religious images, beliefs, and sacred texts keep deep memories alive so that they create a certain paralysis. In essence, the circumstances of Jews living under Islamic rule have created a memory for Muslims that is distinct from that of Jews. Muslims believe that they were the best rulers over minorities, whereas Jews believe they were unfairly treated as second-class citizens under Islamic rule.

During the classical centuries of Islam, persecution of *dhimmis*[9] was very rare. In fact, only one case has been recorded. In 1009, Fatimid caliph al-Hakim (r. 996–1021) ordered the destruction of the Holy Sepulcher in Jerusalem. In the late Middle Ages, however, there was a general hardening of attitudes against *dhimmi*s in Muslim countries. In the West, the Almohads adopted an intolerant policy, while in the East, the government of the Mamluk state could not resist the pressure of jurists, such as Ibn Taymiyya, who insisted on an increasingly troublesome interpretation of the law regarding *dhimmi*s. The legal system of the expanding Ottoman Empire in the sixteenth century finally restored the classical Islamo-*dhimmi* symbiosis. This respite lasted until the middle of the nineteenth century when, under strong European pressure, the provisions of Islamic law were increasingly replaced by new legislation that was intended to free non-Muslims from their inferior status of "protected people" and to make them full citizens. Today, most Constitutions of Muslim states confirm the principle of equality for all citizens, irrespective of religion, sex, and race. Certain militant Islamic groups, however, advocate for the reimposition of the *Jizya*[10] and the *dhimma* regulations (Franke 2004, 451–452).

Islam attempted to allot full rights of justice and equality for minorities, but these rights had actually been founded during Prophet Mohammed's time (*Peace be upon him*). Prophet Mohammed (*Peace be upon him*) was a man who gave rights to women and slaves. Unfortunately, the human rights that were allotted to minorities and women at that time have been swept under the malaise of Islamic practice today. The imposition of certain dress, laws, and restrictions on minorities—especially women—are new laws that extremists want to impose. In other words, a reimposition of a stricter form of the *dhimmi* status has been instituted by certain groups like Boko Haram and ISIS or ISIL (Islamic State of Iraq and Levant) in the past couple of years. For example, the return of the Caliphate period, which ISIL proclaims, is a regression to literalism. It imposes even harsher rules and laws than one can find in early Islam. It seems that the crisis of modernity within some Muslim countries has led to a puritanical type of Islam, one that has forgotten the early societal concerns and rights of minorities.[11]

How Jews and Muslims remember one another, from early Islam to the present, is an important issue that needs to be addressed. Memory can be presented with the nostalgic ease of an untarnished religion or with painful recollections of mistrust and fear of each other. Such deep memory can only be reassessed by people who are willing to take a more profound self-critical view of their traditions and their responses to other traditions. From 9/11 to *Charlie Hebdo*, extremist Muslims have already created new memories that are damaging and painful. Their extreme acts vilify the many heroic acts of Muslims worldwide. If religiously motivated violence troubles us today, then it is essential to analyze how we have reached this point and how we can use consecrated memories to improve relations between Jews and Muslims today.

Notes

1. "France to present Malian Hero with Citizenship," by Alicia Maule www.msnbc.com/msnbc/france-present-malian-hero-citizenship (retrieved March 5, 2015).
2. Trace is neither linear nor chronological. "This trace relates no less to what is called the future than what is called the past, and it constitutes what is called the present by the very relation to what it is not, to what it absolutely is not; that is, not even to a past or future considered as a modified present" (Derrida 1978, 394).
3. On the debate about whether ISIS is Islamic or not, see Graeme Wood, "What ISIS Really Wants," *Atlantic Monthly* (www.theatlantic.com/features/archive/2015/02/what-isis-really-wants/384980/), and Caner K. Dagli, "The Phony Islam of ISIS," *Atlantic Monthly* (www.theatlantic.com/international/archive/2015/02/what-muslims-really-want-isis-atlantic/386156/)
4. Bernard Lewis, "Roots of Muslim Rage," *Atlantic Monthly* (1990) http://www.theatlantic.com/magazine/archive/1990/09/the-roots-of-muslim-rage/304643/ (retrieved April 12, 2015).
5. Samuel Huntington, "The Clash of Civilizations," *Foreign Affairs* (Summer 1993) http://www.foreignaffairs.com/articles/48950/samuel-p-huntington/the-clash-of-civilizations (retrieved April 12, 2015).
6. Reuven Firestone, "Jewish-Muslim Relations," *Modern Judaism* (Oxford Guide) 03/01/04 www.usc.edu/org/cmje/articles/jewish-muslim-relations.php (retrieved March 5, 2015).
7. Khalil Mohammad demonstrates how certain contextual verses in the Qur'an can become problematic and transfixed for some Muslim communities in terms of perceiving the "other."
8. Firestone, www.usc.edu/org/cmje/articles/jewish-muslim-relations.php (retrieved March 5, 2015).
9. *Dhimmi* (protected) was the name and status applied by the Arab-Muslim conquerors to non-Muslim populations who surrendered by a treaty (*dhimma*) to Muslim domination. Muslim empires accommodated numerous people who had their own religion, culture, language, and civilization.
10. *Jizya* is a tax levied upon non-Muslims living under Muslim empires.
11. "List of Islamic Terror Attacks on Christians," www.thereligionofpeace.com/Pages/ChristianAttacks.htm (retrieved April 10, 2015).

Works Cited

Ahmed, Leila, 2000, A Border Passage from Cairo to America—A Woman's Journey, New York: Penguin Books.

Brill, Alan, 2012, Judaism and World Religions: Encountering Christianity, Islam and Eastern Traditions, New York: Palgrave MacMillan.

Cavanaugh, William T., 2009, The Myth of Religious Violence: Secular Ideology and the Roots of Modern Conflict, Oxford: Oxford University Press.

Derrida, Jacques, 1978, Writing and Difference. Trans, Alan Bass, London & New York: Routledge.

Firestone, Reuven, 2008, An Introduction to Islam for Jews, Philadelphia: Jewish Publication Society.

Franke, Patrick, 2004, "Minorities: Dhimmis," in Richard C. Martin ed., Encyclopedia of Islam and the Muslim World, vol. 2, New York: Macmillan Reference, pp. 451–2.

Humphreys, Stephen R., 1999, Between Memory and Desire: The Middle East in a Troubled Age, California: University of California Press.

Jikeli, Gunther, 2015, European Muslim Antisemitism: Why Young Urban Males Say They Don't Like Jews, Bloomington: Indiana University Press.

Khalil, Mohammad, 2012, Islam and the Fate of Others: The Salvation Question, New York: Oxford University Press.

Langer, Lawrence, 1991, Holocaust Testimonies: Ruins of Memory, New Haven: Yale University Press.

Shavit, Ari, 2013, My Promised Land: The Triumph and Tragedy of Israel, New York: Spiegel & Grau.

Wasserstrom, Steven, 1995, Between Muslim and Jew: The Problem of Symbiosis under Early Islam, New Jersey: Princeton University Press.

CROSSCURRENTS

SHIFTING HIERARCHIES OF EXCLUSION[1]
Colonialism, Anti-Semitism, and Islamophobia in European History

Ethan B. Katz

On January 13, 2015, France's Prime Minister Manuel Valls addressed the French National Assembly. He spoke in the wake of the previous week's murderous attacks in Paris by radical Islamists, first at the satirical publication *Charlie Hebdo* and then two days later at the kosher supermarket Hyper Cacher. In his address, Valls received a standing ovation when he declared: "I don't want there to be Jews in our country who are afraid, or Muslims who are ashamed."[2] At this moment, the prime minister and French parliament appeared to recognize the interwoven fates of France's two largest ethno-religious minorities—and of the ideologies of anti-Semitism and Islamophobia.

More than most commentators have realized, such interconnections have a long history, particularly in the Francophone orbit. Much of that history is bound up with the history of colonialism. This essay seeks to begin to understand how colonialism shaped, utilized, and manifested itself in anti-Semitism and Islamophobia from the mid-nineteenth to the mid-twentieth century. For precise historical reasons, we will focus on the French empire, particularly French Algeria.

---

[1] The initial version of this article was prepared as a talk at Brown University given in March 2014. I would like to thank Maud Mandel for the invitation to Brown, where I benefited from discussing these issues with colleagues and students. I was able to explore the issues here further at the symposium "Muslims and Jews: Challenging the Dynamics of Hate," to which I was invited to participate at Northern Arizona University, Flagstaff, AZ, October 5–7, 2014. I remain grateful to the organizers for their invitation and to my colleagues there for good fellowship and fruitful discussion.

This is a history in three stages. In the first stage, the mid-to-late nineteenth century, Islamophobia became much more pronounced in the colonial venture than anti-Semitism. Although Jews' position was never entirely secure, in certain instances they even benefited from colonial rule. By the period between the two World Wars, anti-Semitism had gained growing ferocity across Europe, in France included, while the colonial venture had reached its peak. Both Jews and Muslims were frequently depicted with highly racialized imagery and in many instances faced significant legal and social discrimination. At the same time, Muslims in particular were often the target of propaganda campaigns meant to win their loyalty for one European power or another, as well as provocations meant to turn them against Jews. In the third stage, during the Second World War, the increasing violence of European anti-Semitism crystallized in the horrors of the Holocaust. Muslims, meanwhile, found their position remarkably elevated as Europe's colonial powers struggled to maintain control and as political forces of all stripes saw in Muslims a possible constituency for their wartime aims.

Colonialism's attraction to anti-Semitism and Islamophobia
The Enlightenment and the French Revolution introduced a series of powerful claims about the existence of the nation-state, popular sovereignty, the public "good," and, more broadly, universal principles by which polities should be organized. In the nineteenth century, countries like France and England were at once struggling at home with how far these principles should extend and expanding their imperial power abroad. Exercising colonial rule, while claiming to uphold some version of liberal ideals of universalized citizenship, forced European powers to face the question of how far the new notions of rights and equality might extend into their empires.[3]

Ultimately, by definition, the colony could not become home to universal rights. Settler colonies like Algeria attracted colonists in significant part because of the distinctly unequal opportunities that they offered to Europeans for economic and political power. Moreover, only if Europe was considered superior and the colonized world inferior could the so-called civilizing mission—the frequently invoked notion, in pursuit of colonial conquests, that Europe had an obligation to bring the light of progress and civilization to darker, more primitive parts of the world—have any compelling logic.[4]

More intangible factors served to essentialize the colonized, including Muslims and Jews, in the nineteenth-century European mind. These included long-standing, ubiquitous Orientalist images and associations that exoticized both groups. For many Europeans, the disproportionate fascination with Muslims and Jews meant that these groups were at once different and alluring, uncivilized, and intriguing as possible targets of the civilizing mission.[5] The frequently close relationship, both practical and ideological, between colonialism and European missionary work also lent itself to a particular focus on Muslims and Jews; both had been long-standing objects of European Christian religious hostility, fascination, and conversion fantasies. Finally, it is hardly a coincidence that the era of great colonial expansion in the last decades of the nineteenth century was also the era of the rise of racial thinking. A growing number of philosophers, political leaders, and experts in eugenics and "race science" articulated ideas about so-called white European superiority and the inferiority of allegedly darker-skinned peoples, with Jews and Muslims often included in the latter categories.

France's empire, more than any other, governed over large numbers of Jews and Muslims, often in the same lands, for well over a century. France took a particular interest in each of these populations in a manner connected closely to its own projects of nation- and empire-building. The case of French Algeria is of particular interest because the territory, for most of the period from 1830 to 1962, was not merely a colonial possession, but was actually a part of France itself. This meant that the contradictions of France as a universalist republic and a global empire played out with unusual immediacy in Algeria. Frequently, Jews and Muslims lived such contradictions particularly vividly. Furthermore, French Algeria offers a striking instance of the inseparability of attitudes toward Muslims and Jews, respectively.

1870: The Crémieux decree as hierarchy of exclusion

On October 24, 1870, with the so-called Crémieux Decree, nearly all of Algeria's 37,000 Jews became full French citizens. The act was called after its leading advocate, Adolphe Crémieux, a prominent French lawyer, a major figure in the French-Jewish community, and the Minister of Justice in the French government of the time. This moment crystallized a growing hierarchy of exclusion in nineteenth-century Algeria, wherein the French administration came to favor greater rights for Jewish natives than Muslim natives.

It was not clear that Jews would be favored at the outset. Shortly following the invasion of 1830, French officials created three systems of law. The colonizers would be governed by French law and administrators; both Jews and Muslims would remain under the jurisdiction of their own religious law and courts. In particular with regard to family and religious questions, this remained the case for decades. Meanwhile, during the early years of French conquest in Algeria, French officials frequently spoke ill of the native Jews. Leading French general Thomas-Robert Bugeaud even proposed the removal of Jews from the cities, and longingly exclaimed, "Oh that we could replace through this means, or by another, the Jewish population!" (quoted in Schreier 2010, 49).[6]

Nonetheless, French officials also began to see that they might benefit from seeking to partner with Algerian Jews. In part, they followed the direction of mainland French Jewry. In 1842, with the help of the War Ministry, the official communal apparatus of French Jews, the Central Consistory, sent a fact-finding mission to Algeria. The report of the mission concluded that Algerian Jews, while living in poverty, could be "regenerated" and could also be useful in the project of French domination. In 1845, the Consistory founded branches in Algiers, Constantine, and Oran. During the ensuing two decades, French-Jewish leaders and representatives sought to modernize and Europeanize the lifestyle, practices, and outlook of Algerian Jewry, and to lobby the French government for their emancipation. We should note that sentiments among Algerian Jews were far more resistant, often producing heated conflict between metropolitan consistorial representatives and those they sought to "Frenchify."

Throughout the nineteenth century, colonial and French-Jewish reformers saw the family as a crucial index of sophistication and civilization for Algerian natives. In the 1842 report from the fact-finding mission to Algeria, and repeatedly thereafter, French-Jewish reformers and their allies drew sharp contrasts between stereotypes of veiled, domesticated, separated, unexposed Arab Muslim woman beyond the reach of civilization, and the increasingly free, open, educated, and civilized Algerian

Jewish girl. Legislators, Jewish reformers, and legal theorists alike identified Jewish and Islamic family law as the greatest obstacle to the naturalization of Algerian natives. Indeed, colonial lawmakers and reformers repeatedly invoked Jews' and Muslims' alleged inability or unwillingness to accept the distinction between civil and religious law. This context proved crucial to the July 14, 1865 *senatus-consulte*. This new law made all Algerian natives French "nationals" and stipulated that an individual Jew or Muslim could become a French citizen, but that in order to do so, he had to abandon his Jewish or Muslim "personal status," that is, his right to be governed by Jewish or Muslim law in matters of family and religious life. Very few Muslims or Jews elected to take this step.

Debates about Jews' readiness for naturalization ultimately resolved with the 1870 Crémieux Decree that gave them citizenship and placed them fully under French jurisdiction. For many Jews in Algeria, the change was neither expected nor welcome. Yet in the ensuing decades, widespread attendance at French public schools, mandatory military conscription, economic upward mobility, and correspondent shifts in residential patterns all caused growing numbers of Algerian Jews to either abandon their traditional North African customs or confine them largely to private spaces like the home, and to embrace Frenchness as their primary national (and often cultural) identity (see Friedman 1988).

The Crémieux Decree had no equivalent among Algeria's Muslims, for whom the late nineteenth century proceeded very differently. The decades following the decree saw the rise of an anti-Muslim—and indeed anti-Semitic—"Latin" identity in significant facets of the European settler society of Algeria. This was shaped in large part by the territory's large population of immigrants from Spain, Italy, and Malta (see Lorcin 2002).

One of the key events in the political radicalization of large segments of the settler class and political administration in Algeria was the 1871 Mokrani Revolt. Only months after the Crémieux Decree, the northern mountainous region of Kabylia witnessed a fierce if brief guerilla uprising led by a local sheikh, Mohamed El-Mokrani. The revolt was crushed brutally by the French and in the years and decades to follow, the French expanded, systematized, and made more violent their colonial presence. The European settlers and colonial administration, meanwhile, were deeply alarmed by this sign of resistance from the colonized. Many settlers and colonial officials were certain it was the fault of the Crémieux Decree itself—a belief without foundation—and also saw in Jewish emancipation the haunting prospect of all other native Algerians (i.e. Muslims) gaining equality as well.

From this period until World War II, anti-Semitism would remain a constant in the mainstream of Algerian political life. This stemmed from an effort to deny that Jews could really be "Frenchified" and to question their belonging to a ruling cast primarily made of those of Catholic and "Latin" origins. The European settler classes, moreover, increasingly saw the metropolitan administration as out of touch with their needs and sought to make French Algeria in their own conservative image, viewing it as a kind of *tabula rasa* onto which their fantasies could be projected.[7]

The connections drawn by many European colonists between Jews and Muslims in Algeria at this moment are highly revealing of the relationship between Islamophobia and anti-Semitism. The belief that jealous Muslims fomented the Mokrani Revolt as a protest against the unfairness of the Crémieux Decree offers an initial example of what would become repeatedly articulated European fears that Jews and Muslims were always at odds, seen by many as primitive, tribal peoples ready to do battle with one another like their Biblical ancestors. From an early date, Jewish and Muslim rights were often connected in the minds of Europeans.

Despite France's official goals of "assimilating" the native population of Algeria, the late nineteenth century witnessed a series of measures that created increasingly unbridgeable divides between the colony's European colonizers and the Muslim colonized. In 1881, the French administration created the special *code de l'indigénat*, or "Native Code," consisting of extremely harsh penalties for violation of thirty-three separate restrictions imposed solely on native Muslims. Meanwhile, with the French citizenship law of 1889, all "Europeans" of Algeria became full French citizens. The administration continued to dismantle long-standing tribally and communally based property systems, expropriating millions of acres of farmland; and it placed extreme tax burdens upon native Muslims.

To be sure, we see here that in the late nineteenth-century colonial context, Jews were seen by the French state and society as more capable than Muslims of being "civilized." In the hierarchy of exclusion so crucial to the colonial context, Islamophobia proved far more absolute at this time than anti-Semitism. And yet, nonetheless, the elevation of Jews over Muslims, particularly in Algeria, was ever fragile and hotly contested.

This was never clearer than during the anti-Semitic outbreaks that occurred at the fin-de-siècle during the Dreyfus Affair. In May 1897, in the port city of Mostaganem, in the middle of a cycling race, a fight broke out that resulted in Europeans and Muslims attacking the Jewish quarter. Max Régis, the new president of the anti-Jewish League and the future mayor of the capital city of Algiers (he was elected the following year), directed his supporters to go into the Jewish section of Algiers and chant "Long live the Army! Down with the Jews!" More than 100 were injured, and Jewish stores were looted. There were eventually riots across Algeria that targeted Jews (Benbassa 1999, 145).

It was at this moment that anti-Semitism really took hold in Algerian political life. Régis founded a newspaper called *L'Anti-Juif*, which was inspired by the ideas of notorious anti-Semitic author Edouard Drumont, who had written the infamous screed *La France Juive* [The Jewish France]. The newspaper achieved a fairly large print-run for its time of about 20,000. Drumont himself was elected a deputy to the National Assembly from the 2nd district of Algiers in 1898; three other candidates of the same party won in Algiers, Oran, and Constantine, giving the anti-Semitic party four of Algeria's six members in the Chamber of Deputies at this time. The city of Oran elected a majority-anti-Semitic municipal council for the first time, setting the tone for its local politics for decades. During the Dreyfus Affair, even some Algerian Muslims, previously calm in the face of anti-Semitic provocations, became hostile and attacked Jews (Abitbol 1990, 209–210, Benbassa 1999).

World War I as a critical turning point

From 1914 to 1918, in the course of the First World War, over 800,000 subjects came to France from across the empire to fight on the battlefield or work on the home front. Nearly 400,000 North African Muslims, comprising 260,000 soldiers and over 130,000 laborers, made up a strong plurality of these colonial soldiers and laborers. Meanwhile, 38,000 Jews from France and North Africa fought for the French armed forces.[8] Many members of both groups saw the war as an opportunity to further or complete their integration into the French nation. In many respects, this proved simpler for Jews than for Muslims, given the former's long-standing presence in France, their centralized communal structure, and their high levels of acculturation into French society. That is, if Jewish service was an affirmation of their belonging in France, for Muslims, it constituted more of a plea for basic recognition and rights (for a fuller discussion of Jews, Muslims, and their relations in France during World War I, see Katz 2015).

And yet the division was neither so stark nor so simple. First of all, despite France's vaunted "Sacred Union" of Catholics, Protestants, and Jews, and Jews' evident and fervent wartime patriotism, anti-Semitism hardly disappeared during the war. The summer of 1915 saw a wave of accusations about France's Russian Jewish immigrants shirking their duty; many subsequently chose not to enlist or even fled the country. In the course of the war, more than 150 publications appeared in France attacking such alleged subversive forces as Jewish-German spies or the Jewish-Masonic conspiracy. Meanwhile, during the war, on the one hand, French officials and politicians were observing firsthand that Muslims from French North Africa offered powerful possibilities for fulfilling various aspects of nation- and empire-building; on the other hand, as hundreds of thousands of Muslims fought under the French colors and carried French arms, their service alongside French citizens and "whites" challenged basic colonial hierarchies.

Meanwhile, broader developments of World War I would help to shape attitudes and practices toward Jews and Muslims for decades. First, the end of the Ottoman Empire brought millions of Muslims under European control in what would become the British and French Mandates; in this context, the British made promises to both Jews and Arabs that turned Palestine into a fiercely contested territory with transnational implications. This gave a new urgency to competing European efforts to curry favor with significant parts of the Muslim world, leading to substantial propaganda campaigns, particularly in the 1930s. The Palestine Mandate also heightened the sense of inevitable Jewish–Muslim conflict as a consideration in domestic and imperial politics. Secondly, the untold violence of the war and its profoundly destabilizing effects on European society, politics, and economy helped to unleash what George L. Mosse famously called the "brutalization of politics." Through this dynamic, political violence of language and physical attack became far more accepted, ideas of exclusionary, racial nationhood spread beyond a small faction on the extreme right, and fascist movements with paramilitary wings came to the fore, including in France by the 1930s (Mosse 1990).

The rise of fascism and World War II

By the 1930s, extremist political groups of the far-right began to proliferate. The question of Jews' and Muslims' place in the French polity became hotly debated in this period, particularly in the contexts of two major issues: the question of the future of French Algeria; and the struggle between fascism and anti-fascism in France. For all their differences, the far-right groups that came to prominence in France and more so Algeria had much in common. All focused on veterans and the experience of World War I; all articulated an ardent, often xenophobic nationalism; all supported traditional social hierarchies; all were fiercely anti-communist; and all had ambitions to replace republican democracy with an authoritarian system. The far right had an impact on Jewish–Muslim relations largely through the two largest quasi-fascist movements of the period, the *Croix-de-Feu* (CDF) and from 1936 onward the *Parti Populaire Français* (PPF).[9]

The CDF, whose membership reached 700,000 to a million members by the late 1930s, had a tortured relationship with Jews. On the one hand, within the group, financial backer Ernest Mercier, leading activist Ferdinand Robbe, and more than a few members were Jewish. From 1932 to 1936, with approval from the Paris Consistory, the CDF took part in religious ceremonies at Parisian synagogues to honor Jewish veterans of the Great War. On repeated occasions until the late 1930s, party leader Lieutenant Colonel François de la Rocque publicly rejected anti-Semitism. At the same time, local sections of the CDF, particularly in Algeria, sought to stir up anti-Jewish sentiment. By 1935, some party activists in Algeria entered Jewish neighborhoods to chant "Long live La Rocque" and "Long live Hitler." Despite ardently defending the inequalities of colonial society, the league recruited numerous Muslims in Algeria; frequently CDF activists attempted to win Muslims over with anti-Semitism. The CDF and other right-wing groups were accused of helping to foment the greatest episode of Jewish–Muslim violence in the French empire during the inter-war period, the riots of Constantine in Algeria in August 1934, which left 25 Jews and 4 Muslims dead (Cole 2010).

It was in this context that on April 4, 1936, the popular Jewish anti-racist organization, the *Ligue Internationale Contre l'Antisémitisme* (LICA), ran a satirical cartoon on the front of its newspaper *Le droit de vivre*, targeting the *Croix-de-Feu*. The cartoon features the group's leader de la Rocque as a Janus speaking to both Muslims and Jews. To the Muslims, he declares: "The Frenchman is not your oppressor; your enemy is the Jew, who robs you and ruins you." To the Jewish audience, he exclaims, "A wave of anti-Semitism would be disastrous for our country."[10] The words here were actual quotations from different CDF leaflets distributed in Algeria.

In the face of the rising menace of fascism in France, a counter-mobilization occurred as well, in the form of a left-wing coalition that became known as the Popular Front, bringing together the Socialist and Communist Parties, the centrist Radical Party, and many allied associations and interest groups. This group won the May 1936 parliamentary elections; its head Léon Blum, leader of the Socialist Party and a proud Jew, became prime minister. As if the rise of a left-wing government headed by a Jew of the Socialist Party were not enough, in his early months in office, Blum teamed with reformist former Governor-General Maurice Viollet, hated by Algerian colonists, to propose the Blum-Viollette bill, which would have given full French citizenship to over 20,000 Algerian Muslims. Following the Popular Front's victory, as factory strikes erupted across not only France but also Algeria in June 1936, often with ample Muslim participation, the right-wing ideologues of French Algeria thought they were living their worst nightmare. A wave of anti-Semitic violence, already brewing in the preceding months in Algeria, now erupted in full fury. In the far-right stronghold of Oran, on June 26, members of the CDF trashed the inside of a local bar as they chanted anti-communist slogans. They then proceeded to the Jewish quarter, yelling "Down with the Jews," "Blum to the gallows!" and "Long live fascism!" (Kalman 2013, 116). Such incidents quickly became commonplace. Fears of Jewish power, Muslim revolt, and leftist reform became unified into a single movement of political violence.[11] Anti-Semitism was in the lead, but Islamophobia was quite present as well.

It was in the period following the election of the Popular Front that the second large far-right party, Jacques Doriot's *Parti Populaire Français* (PPF), was formed and began its own recruitment of Muslims. As the Popular Front government collapsed, and along with it hopes for the Blum-Viollette reform, many Muslim activists who had placed their hopes in the anti-fascist coalition became deeply disillusioned. The PPF, which had exhibited its own ambiguous relationship to Jews in the early years, became more decisively anti-Semitic following the death of Jewish leading party member David Abramski in February 1937. Soon, its platform in Algeria declared "North Africa must be totally freed from Jewish control" (Soucy 1995, 278).

By the late 1930s, then, the far right in France and Algeria felt threatened enough by the prospect of a leftist–Jewish–Muslim alliance that it concentrated its greatest hatred on the Jews, perceived as uniquely powerful and serving as a convenient and increasingly popular scapegoat. Such conceptions reached their zenith, of course, with the Vichy regime during the Second World War. The period confirmed in the most tragic way possible that anti-Semitism was now far more central for the French state and society than Islamophobia. Jews, of course, officially became "non-Aryans," and faced a series of lethal anti-Semitic measures from Vichy and the Nazis. In Algeria, all Jews lost their French citizenship in autumn 1940. Yet, Muslims in France and North Africa—even though most still lacked French citizenship—became racially akin to "Aryans."[12]

The latter development, if seemingly counter-intuitive, reflected strategic choices on the part of both Vichy and the Nazis, as the French state and its occupiers competed fiercely over the future of French North Africa and the broader empire. In the course of the war, the Vichy regime and leading French collaborationist political parties like the PPF reached out to Muslims, giving Islam newfound prominence in the French public sphere, and recruiting Muslim support. In this context, certain Muslims elected to promote their own position—to combat Islamophobia as it were—by embracing the politics of anti-Semitism.

On March 29, 1942, for instance, a large PPF meeting took place in Paris focused on "French Imperial Unity," and three leading Muslim members of the PPF, Sheikh Mohamed Zouani, Mostefa Bendjamaa, and Si Ahmed Belghoul, traveled from Algeria to address the gathering. As they stood at the lectern, behind the speakers, beneath an enormous image of party leader Doriot, were written Arabic words that translate as: "Our policy: governing with justice; respecting religions, and partnering in the general welfare." The phrase echoed the PPF's imperial motto of "Rule, Respect, Associate," part of a policy platform that was deeply committed to empire and its hierarchies, but that offered Muslims and other colonized natives greater autonomy and respect for their cultural and religious traditions and institutions. Before a crowd of 800, including

350–400 Muslims, all three Muslim leaders delivered impassioned speeches. Bendjamaa, in particular, articulated a markedly exclusionary religious politics. He exclaimed: "God tells us in our Quran: 'the greatest enemy of Islam, it is the Jew.'" He lamented that "Jews at any price want to destroy Islam," and linked Judaism with Communism as a "two-headed serpent" that Muslims had to fight.[13]

Of course, this meeting was hardly the norm for Muslim political activism during the war. Lest we be left with the mistaken impression that most Muslims in the French empire during World War II were anti-Semitic fascists, we should note that, despite weeks of feverish publicity, this meeting only attracted a few hundred Muslim participants among the tens of thousands living in the French capital at that time. Moreover, those who did support the Nazis, Vichy, or collaboration often did so for motivations other than anti-Semitism. Anti-colonialism or the hope that the Germans or Vichy would be better masters than the governments of the Third Republic were among the most common factors.

Inseparable hatreds

Through the historical period surveyed here, we can observe a process of evolution. In French colonial hierarchies of exclusion where both anti-Semitism and Islamophobia figured prominently, it was first Islamophobia in the nineteenth century that seemed most important; then following World War I, a kind of competition between Islamophobia and anti-Semitism within extremist right-wing politics emerged; and then, the Second World War saw the tragic resolution of this competition in the Holocaust and a surprisingly promising political environment for Muslims. At no time were anti-Semitism or Islamophobia entirely separate from one another. Rather, they were often mutually reinforcing, either through policies of divide-and-rule or through the heightened fears they produced about both Jews and Muslims and their combined danger on the part of French authorities and right-wing political groups. In the decades since the Second World War, and particularly since the 1980s, despite their persistent nostalgia for the Vichy period and their profound discomfort with the memory of the Holocaust, far-right parties like the *Front National* have made Islamophobic anti-immigrant sentiment far more central to their politics than anti-Semitism.[14] Nonetheless, it bears remembering today that when the rhetoric of either anti-Semitism or Islamophobia is invoked, whichever remains unmentioned is often present in the uncomfortable silence.

Notes

2. "Valls: 'Je ne veux pas que des juifs puissent avoir peur ou des musulmans puissent avoir honte," *L'Obs*, January 13, 2005, online at http://tempsreel.nouvelobs.com/charlie-hebdo/20150113.OBS9899/valls-je-ne-veux-pas-que-des-juifs-puissent-avoir-peur-ou-des-musulmans-puissent-avoir-honte.html.
3. On the particular contradictions of modern European colonialism, I have been influenced by Cooper and Stoler (1997).
4. For what remain deeply insightful observations along these lines, see Memmi (1965).
5. For a good overview regarding Muslims, see Hourani (1991); on Jews in Enlightenment and revolutionary France as "good to think," see Schechter (2003).
6. On these issues broadly (here and in the next two paragraphs), see Schreier (2010).
7. On the development of anti-Semitism in Algeria during this period, Dermenjian (1986); on its place within a wider increasingly authoritarian ideology, Kalman (2013).
8. Regarding Muslims and other colonial soldiers in the war, I have relied on Fogarty (2008); regarding Jews, Landau (2000).
9. For a good discussion of the Croix-de-Feu, see Irvine (1991).
10. "La Rocque-Janus," cartoon in *Le Droit de Vivre*, April 4, 1936.
11. See esp. Chapter 3 in Kalman (2013).
12. For much more detailed discussion of all the complex developments mentioned in this section, see chapter 3 in Katz (2015).
13. "Le P.P.F. a réuni hier à Magic City des milliers de musulmans et de français," *Le Cri du Peuple*, 30 March 1942.
14. On the shift away from anti-Semitism on the French far right in the postwar decades, see Vinen (1994).

Works Cited

Abitbol, Michel, 1990, "La Citoyenneté Imposée: Du Décret Crémieux à la guerre d'Algérie," in Pierre Birnbaum, ed., Histoire Politique des Juifs en France, Paris: Presses de Sciences Po.

Benbassa, Esther, 1999, The Jews of France: A History from Antiquity to the Present, trans. M.B. DeBevoise, Princeton: Princeton University Press.

Cole, Joshua, 2010, "Antisémitisme et situation coloniale pendant l'entre-deux-guerres en Algérie: Les émeutes antijuives de Constantine," Vingtième siècle **108** (October–December), pp. 2–23.

Cooper, Frederick, and Ann Laura Stoler, 1997, "Between Metropole and Colony: Rethinking a Research Agenda," in A. L. Stoler, and F. Cooper eds., Tensions of Empire: Colonial Cultures in a Bourgeois World, Berkeley, CA: University of California Press, pp. 1–53.

Dermenjian, Geneviève, 1986, La crise anti-juive oranaise (1895–1905): L'antisémitisme en Algérie coloniale, Paris: L'Harmattan.

Fogarty, Richard S., 2008, Race and War in France: Colonial Subjects in the French Army, 1914–1918, Baltimore: Johns Hopkins University Press.

Friedman, Elizabeth, 1988, Colonialism & After: An Algerian Jewish Community. Boston: Bergin & Garvey.

Hourani, Albert, 1991, "Islam in European Thought," in Hourani, Islam in European Thought and Other Essays. Cambridge: Cambridge University Press, pp. 7–60.

Irvine, William, 1991, "Fascism in France and the Strange Case of the Croix-de-Feu," The Journal of Modern History **63**(2), pp. 271–95.

Kalman, Samuel, 2013, French Colonial Fascism: The Extreme Right in Algeria, 1919–1939, New York: Palgrave Macmillan.

Katz, Ethan, 2015, The Burdens of Brotherhood: Jews and Muslims from North Africa to France, Cambridge, MA: Harvard University Press.

Landau, Philippe E., 2000, Les Juifs de France et la Grande Guerre: Un patriotisme républicain, 1914–1941, Paris: Editions CNRS.

Lorcin, Patricia M. E., 2002, "Rome and France in Africa: Recovering Colonial Algeria's Latin Past," French Historical Studies **25**(2), pp. 295–329.

Memmi, Albert, 1965, The Colonizer and the Colonized, trans. Howard Greenfeld with a new introduction by the author, preface by Jean-Paul Sartre, New York: Orion Press.

Mosse, George L., 1990, Fallen Soldiers: Reshaping the Memory of the World Wars, Oxford: Oxford University Press.

Schechter, Ronald, 2003, Obstinate Hebrews: Representations of Jews in France, 1715–1815, Berkeley: University of California Press.

Schreier, Joshua, 2010, Arabs of the Jewish Faith: The Civilizing Mission in Colonial Algeria, New Brunswick, NJ: Rutgers University Press.

Soucy, Robert, 1995, French Fascism: The Second Wave, 1933–1939, New Haven: Yale University Press.

Vinen, Richard, 1994, "The End of an Ideology? Right-Wing Antisemitism in France, 1944–1970, The Historical Journal **37**(1), pp. 365–88.

CROSSCURRENTS

OUTLAWING THE VEIL, BANNING THE MUSLIM? RESTRICTING RELIGIOUS FREEDOM IN FRANCE

Melanie Adrian

In the last ten years, France has increasingly limited religious expression by banning ostentatious religious symbols in public schools in 2004 and face coverings in public spaces in 2011. Both of these laws were drafted and enacted after public discussions around the management of rising religious diversity in France—most notably Islam.[1] During these debates, the French openly wondered about differences that impacted or confronted national norms while respecting national values. This included questions around the meaning of secularism—broadly translated as *laïcité*—and the limits of religious manifestation in the public sphere.

In their efforts to maintain a Republican political model, based on a strong public/private divide, the French have, by way of these laws, increasingly required minorities to comply with specific forms of public behavior. Given that some Muslims believe certain types of comportment—such as the veil—is an essential component of their religious obligation, this has required that they choose between their faith and compliance with these laws.

The cost for many has been high, as it has forced them to choose between wearing a veil or being part of French society in the most basic way; it has compromised their ability to live authentically as contributing members of society. They are, in the most practical of ways, cut off from contact. In addition, the conversations around the creation of the law have increased discrimination of Muslims and instigated questions around their ability to integrate and "be French" when many Muslims are already French citizens. Equality, liberty, and toleration are at stake in these conversations.

I will briefly outline a few key points to show that religious freedom has been a central value in France since the late 1700s. Increasing cultural and religious diversity pressed on the limits of *laïcité*, erupting as it did in 1989 in the schools. The reaction since that time has been to relegate the manifestation of religious diversity, and the Muslim veil in particular, into the bounds of the private sphere. This has been supported, I show, by the European Court of Human Rights. But what affect does this have on French Muslims? The last section of this article shows that Muslims feel (and are) increasingly discriminated and are viewed as foreigners in need of integration. This undercuts the values of equality and liberty of the Republic.

Religious freedom in France

For centuries, French thought and legislation have protected religious freedom. It was included, for example, in some of the foundational documents of the Republic, such as the 1789 Declaration of the Rights of Man and the Citizen.[2] Since that time, the French have increasingly nuanced the place of religion. In the 1800s and early 1900s, this meant a sustained reflection of the influence of the Catholic Church on the religious, political, and economic life of the nation.

Thus in the 1880s, Jules Ferry proposed a set of laws that mandated that teachers had to be laypersons and that religion be left out of the curriculum (see Bowen 2007, p. 25). By these acts and others, French society gradually distanced its social and political institutions from the Church and religion more generally. This protected an individual's right to freedom of conscience while also progressively circumscribing religion to the private sphere.

The relationship between religion and social institutions would be officially enshrined in the oft-mentioned law of 1905. This law states in part:

> Article 1: The Republic assures freedom of conscience. It guarantees freedom of worship, with restrictions hereafter only in the interest of public order.
>
> Article 2: The Republic does not recognize, provide employment in or subsidy to any religion... (Baubérot and Dagens 2005, p. 64)

The law envisioned a detachment of state from religion by allowing private citizens to form religious associations that would serve as intermediaries between religion and the state. The idea was to separate the public and private spheres in order to protect religious freedom (among other freedoms) in a space apart while at the same time shielding common norms of equality and liberty in the Republic. The approach followed the thinking of Jean-Jacques Rousseau (1987), whereby the citizen was foremost cast along political lines when they stepped out into the public sphere. Here, it was thought, they could disengage their personal affiliations and act befitting the collective good. The central tension with this approach is when private beliefs—or identity—bleed into the public sphere.

As a final point of emphasis, in the most recent Constitution, religious freedom is addressed in article 1, which states, in part:

> France shall be an indivisible, secular, democratic and social Republic. It shall ensure the equality of all citizens before the law, without distinction of origin, race or religion. It shall respect all beliefs....[3]

This prominence on religious freedom throughout the centuries has meant that there is little controversy around the freedom to practice religion in private in France. Individuals can observe religious obligations and eat, drink, and pursue ritual broadly. The controversy begins at the doorstep to the public sphere, especially for those who believe they are required to wear a headscarf in public spaces in order to meet the stipulations of their faith. This has become a point of contention in part because some believe the headscarf infringes on the definition of what it means to have a secular public sphere. This was keenly felt in public schools, which have been the beacons of secularism since the time of Ferry.

The issue around headscarves in schools began, as is well known, in 1989. At the beginning of that school year, three young women came to school wearing their headscarves. The school administrations balked at this because schools, they believed, were meant to provide a secular education and a neutral space for learning—free from personal commitments. This incident reignited a national debate around the status of *laïcité* and what role religion should play in public. The stakes were high as the terms had been long debated and fought for.

After a few years of contention around these issues, President Chirac called a Commission to investigate the status of *laïcité* in France. This Commission, called the Stasi Commission,[4] made 26 recommendations, including the proposal to draft a law banning religious garb in public schools.

The law was passed a few months later and banned ostentatious religious symbols, including veils, in public schools across the country. Although the law was written in a generalized way in order to conform to the equality clauses, the Muslim communities observed—quite rightly from my perspective—that this was a conversation targeted at them. The few hundred schoolgirls who wore the veil would now have to choose between this religious expression and attending public school.[5]

In 2011, in a slightly different political climate, the French passed another law that directly affected Muslim women when they banned face coverings in public. For the minority of women who choose to wear the face veil along with the headscarf, this meant that they were (and are) prohibited from entering government buildings, walking down the street, taking a bus, and dropping their children off at school.

Taken together, these two laws restrict Muslim women who choose to veil from attending public schools and, if they don the face veil, being part of the public sphere. They must decide for either one or the other. At what cost, however, does this restriction of religious freedom come for those who understand the veil as an important expression of their religious identity? What happens to their understanding of religious obligation and their duo identity as French and Muslim? More generally, what is the cost to the rest of society of freedom, equality, and toleration? Before attempting to answer these questions, it is important to understand whether this type of restriction is simply the cost of living in France, or whether this is part of a wider European approach.

Religious freedom in Europe: The case of SAS v. France

The European Court of Human Rights recently had the opportunity to examine the French law banning face coverings in public. On the day the law was brought into force, a French national (born in Pakistan) brought the case to the European Court of Human Rights. Although never arrested, she held that the law "deprived her of the possibility of wearing the full face veil in public."[6] She argued that this was contrary to her right to religious freedom.

In a judgment handed down in July of 2014, the Court ruled in favor of the French government. They found that the face veil contravened "'respect for the minimum requirements of life in society' – or of 'living together'."[7] They held the face is an important marker of social interaction that, if hidden, contravenes the rights of others to live in a space of socialization which makes living together easier. The wording the Court used is important here:

> ...the face plays an important role in social interaction. [The Court] can understand the view that individuals who are present in places open to all may not wish to see practices or attitudes developing there which would fundamentally call into question the possibility of open interpersonal relationships, which, by virtue of an established consensus, forms an indispensable element of community life within the society in question. The Court is therefore able to accept that the barrier raised against others by a veil concealing the face is perceived by... [France] as breaching the right of others to live in a space of socialisation which makes living together easier.[8]

One may agree or disagree with France's law and the European Court's support of the law. One may find the face veil disagreeable, foreign, or uncomfortable. The more general question, however, is how these laws affect the Muslim population and wider conceptions of equality and liberty. What of toleration?

On the point of toleration, the Court expresses concern. Further along in the judgment they address the issue of Islamophobia directly. They "emphasise that [this action risks] contributing to the consolidation of the stereotypes which affect certain categories of the population and of encouraging the expression of intolerance, when it has a duty, on the contrary, to promote tolerance."[9] The Court is right to worry about the effects of this ruling on the discrimination of Muslims. As Farid Hafez argues in his article tracing the interconnections of anti-Semitism with Islamophobia in far right politics in Europe, Islamophobia has largely replaced anti-Semitism. He cites the 2011 European Report on Intolerance that showed that the majority of the population believes that Islam is a religion of intolerance.[10]

How do laws such as these affect Muslims living in France? In 2005–2006, I went to France to ask Muslims (and others) this question. I spent the year researching and teaching English conversation in a public high school just south of Paris. While there, I had the opportunity to speak with, and befriend, a wide variety of Muslims. I asked them directly about how they were affected.

On discrimination and integration

In conversations with my Muslim friends, I took away many riches. I would like to share two reflections that were frequently mentioned by many of the people I spoke with. These everyday experiences shed light on how Muslims in France are treated and how laws that restrict religious freedom affect them.

The first thought is that the women who choose to veil are already—and this is before the passing of the law banning face veils—harassed and discriminated on the streets of France and hence made to feel less than. As Diana explained to me one day at her home over steaming mint tea, people are scared of them: they fear them, they spit at them, and they walk on the other side of the road to avoid them. She said: "When I walk down the street there are people who look at me like I'm nothing." Her sister-in-law Stephanie, who had converted to Islam a few years before and who does not veil in public, added:

> The problem [of unequal treatment] is worse for Muslims because even a very devout practicing Jew or Christian is not going to be denigrated like a Muslim. For Muslims, it's really hard. Look at me, I was scared to tell my family that I had converted. It is as if there was a huge burden to carry and pressure to bear. Being Muslim in France is like being defiled. You are obliged to always prove to people that you have value while everyone else already does. But for them, you really don't have value. I don't know why it's like that, but it is.

Many of my Muslim conversation partners echoed these views. Being Muslim in France automatically balkanizes one into a discreet category of other that is to be at once feared, in need of protection, and seen as opposed to the common norms that bind French society (see also Fernando 2014).

The act of veiling is seen as being opposed to how the public and private are divided, and how *laïcité* is currently interpreted. *Being* Muslim (in private) is not the issue, but *acting* Muslim (in public) is. It is not just, however, the affects on the public sphere and the interpretation of *laïcité*, that is at issue in these debates. It brings up the question of integration and how well Muslims fit into French society. Is it possible to integrate Muslims if they choose different forms of public appearance? What does integration mean, for example, for Abbas, a seventeen-year-old Arab boy I met at school? Abbas' parents came to France from Algeria before he was born. Abbas initially described himself as half Algerian and half French. He explained:

> My parents, they came from Algeria and they educated me in the Algerian ways, just like they were. I am of Algerian culture so I can't say that I'm totally French... No, I am French, but I'm Algerian too. I am completely French, and I'm Algerian too.

As Abbas' statement shows, identity is a complex phenomenon that is not easily framed and can change from life moment to another. At home, he may identify more with certain customs and rituals that are shaped by the culture or religion of Algeria. With his friends at school, he may highlight a different side of who he is. What does integration mean when one identifies with different aspects of being religious, cultural, and political?

What does integration mean for Mohammed, a Muslim who was born and raised in France? Mohammad was a well-loved teacher at the school who sat down to explain to me the difficulty he faces living his faith and pursuing his profession. He struggled with his roles as Muslim, Frenchman, and teacher.

> I feel like I'm in a vise. Why? Because I'm a Muslim, a French Muslim and I pray five times a day... At a certain moment it's just not obvious how I can live my religion...[and be a teacher that upholds the values of] French institutions... I'm like this [acts out to show that his head is pressed in on both sides].

The problem, as Abbas and Mohammad describe it, is that one part of their identity fits uncomfortably (at best) into the public sphere. The more the veil and other religious symbols are banned, the less space there is for people of faith to live authentically as Muslims and Frenchmen. Banning the veil through the passing of the 2004 and 2011 laws has also had the effect of increasingly rendering religion a taboo subject, which is not to be discussed, Mohammad explained.

Before the veil was banned in public schools, he could address issues—such as establishing a room for prayer or the religious dimensions of local conflict—using a variety of lenses, including tradition, culture, and religion. Now that religion has been cast into the private sphere more and more, he is reluctant to have this conversation with his students. He fears the repercussions from his colleagues who see him as not upholding laic principles and his mandate as a teacher in a secular school system. This, they have told him, is his duty as a teacher and citizen and is part of integrating into the French way of life.

Yet, Mohammed was born in France and does not know any other life, but still he is an example of the type of person some see as needing to be integrated because of his strong beliefs in his cultural background, faith, and his desire to pass this on to his children. He feels like he is in a vise—a strong visual image of what is happening to him and other Muslims in France today.

As we can see from these two brief examples, identity and religious manifestation do not fit neatly into the private sphere, be it because of the veil or because humans are by nature complex intercultural beings that are constantly evolving. Those people who engage, perhaps by necessity, their complex selves in the public arena face questions as to their suitability for equal inclusion in the French public sphere. To what extent, however, does this undermine the very definition of equality and liberty that are part of the foundation of the French Republic?

Notes

1. The 2004 law was passed after a recommendation was issued by a Commission of experts (known as the Stasi Commission), which was created to study diversity in France, assembled by then-President Chirac. The 2011 law was passed after a Parliamentary Commission issued a Report on the face veil in France. The subsequent Resolution at the National Assembly was called *Attachment and Respect for Republican Values at a Time when they are Being Undermined by the Development of Radical Practices*.
2. Article 10 in that Declaration states, "no one shall be disquieted on account of his opinions, including his religious views, provided their manifestation does not disturb the public order established by law." http://www.conseil-constitutionnel.fr/conseil-constitutionnel/english/constitution/constitution-of-4-October-1958.25742.html (accessed 19 March 2015).
3. http://www.assemblee-nationale.fr/english/index.asp (accessed 19 March 2015).
4. See Note 1.
5. Sikhs were the second most affected religious group.
6. *SAS v France*, (GC) No. 43835/11 [2014]. Para. 10, 76, 3.

7. *SAS v France*, (GC) No. 43835/11 [2014]. Para. 121.
8. *SAS v France*, (GC) No. 43835/11 [2014]. Para. 122.
9. *SAS v France*, (GC) No. 43835/11 [2014]. Para. 149.
10. Hafez states: "Far right parties with former historical links to fascism or National Socialism have been attempting to distance themselves from their previous antisemitism by positioning themselves as pro-Israeli, while their reliance on the epistemic essence of racialization has only moved from a Jewish to a Muslim subject" (2014, p. 479, 498).

Works Cited

Baubérot, J., and C. Dagens, 2005, La Laïcité en France, Paris: Parole et Silence.

Bowen, J. R., 2007, Why the French Don't Like Headscarves, Princeton: Princeton University Press.

Fernando, M. L., 2014, The Republic Unsettled: Muslim French and the Contradictions of Secularism, Durham: Duke University Press.

Hafez, F., 2014, "Shifting Borders: Islamophobia as Common Ground for Building Pan-European Right-Wing Unity," Patterns of Prejudice **48**(5), pp. 477–499.

Rousseau, J.-J., 1987, The Basic Political Writings, Indianapolis: Hackett Publishing Company.

CROSSCURRENTS

WHEN THE VICTIMS ARE NOT SO INNOCENT
Extremist Muslim Activity in Western Bloc Countries

Khaleel Mohammed

To some observers, the horrific crimes on 9/11 were not just the work of a few Muslim extremists, but rather the culmination of a philosophy preached by a religion bent on world domination. This negative image of Islam and Muslims, however, did not begin on September 11, 2001. Two decades before this event, Edward Said, had observed:

> So far as the United States seems to be concerned, it is only a slight overstatement to say that Arabs and Muslims are essentially seen as either oil suppliers or potential terrorists. Very little of the detail, the human density, the passion of Arab-Moslem life has entered the awareness of even those people whose profession is to report the Arab World. What we have, instead, is a series of crude, essentialized caricatures of the Islamic world, presented in such a way as to make the world vulnerable to military aggression.[1]

In the 1997 reprint of his *Covering Islam,* Said further noted that, "malicious generalizations about Islam have become the last acceptable from of denigration of foreign culture in the West; what is said about the Muslim mind, or character, or religion, or culture as a whole cannot now be said in mainstream discussion about Africans, Jews, other Orientals or Asians" (Said 1997, xii). To add to the egregiousness of this discrimination, Jack Shaheen has documented almost 900 films from the beginning of the cinema industry in the West, starting in 1896, that show how Arabs (read "Muslims") have been constantly portrayed as "brutal, heartless, uncivilized fanatics and money-mad cultural 'others' bent on terrorizing civilized Westerners, especially Christians and Jews" (Shaheen 2003, 172). The recent furor over Donald Trump's failure to correct a supporter who assumed President Obama to be a Muslim, as well as Ben Carson's statement about not voting for a Muslim president only underline the pervasive demonization of Muslims in America.

Anti-Muslim prejudices in the U.S

The word Islamophobia has been widely used to denote such prejudice against Islam. The term came into prominence with the 1997 Runnymede Trust's publication, *Islamophobia: A Challenge for Us All,* although it had been used earlier without much notice (Richardson 1997). In opposition to the Runnymede Trust findings, some popular writers stridently claim that there is no such thing as Islamophobia—arguing that is it perfectly acceptable for people to state their feelings against a faith whose followers commit acts of terror with a goal to world domination.[2] The pervasiveness of the negative depiction in films and news media, however, completely debunks this contention.

In the week after 9/11, Arabs and South Asians reported 645 cases of bias and hate crimes (Cainkar 2002). During 2001, anti-Muslim hate crimes in the United States increased by 1,700 percent. In the hurriedly passed Patriot Act of October 2001, John Ashcroft, the born-again Christian U.S. Attorney General, rounded up 1,200 Arab, South Asian, and Muslim men on suspicion of possible ties to terrorism (Curtis IV 2009, 100). Authorities stopped counting after that number, due to what it termed "statistical confusion" (Abdo 2009, 84). Citing the need for national security, officials refused to release the names of the detainees or to allow them access to lawyers; they held them in custody without charging them with any crimes; in some cases, they refused to even notify their families.

Although the importance of religion is often downplayed in the United States, a *Newsweek* poll in 2009 showed that approximately 62 percent of Americans believed the USA to be a Christian nation. Church leaders have not been reluctant to weigh in with their views of Islam and Muslims.[3] In October 2002, Jerry Falwell, at the time Chancellor and President of Liberty University, the largest private Christian college in the USA, pronounced Muhammad a terrorist, the opposite of Jesus and Moses.[4] Franklin Graham, son of renowned evangelist Billy Graham, called Islam a "violent and evil" religion.[5] He later amended this sentiment to, Islam "is not the faith of this country. And that is not the religion that built this nation. The people of the Christian faith and the Jewish faith are the ones who built America, and it is not Islam."[6] As if the news media and film were not enough to purvey Islamophobia, many Muslims are pointing out that advertisements have been posted on buses in New York City and San Francisco as of January 2015.

Not so innocent: case studies
Unlike many of my coreligionists, however, I view that there are often other realities that must be considered in the face of negative blanket "othering." As such, when I was invited to a conference on "Muslims and Jews: Challenging the Dynamics of Hate" at Northern Arizona University in October 2014, I decided to make a presentation that went against the expected input from a Muslim academic. Having studied or provided expert testimony in several cases involving terrorism and civil action brought against corporations by Muslim litigants, I hold that there are those who, while claiming to be a victimized minority, conduct themselves in a way that often shows them to be not so innocent. I offer the following cases, both civil and criminal, as evidence of my contention. Since they were covered by the popular news media, I have, for ease of reference, used newspaper and television sources as much as possible.

In September 2002, Yahya Goba, Yassein Taher, Sahim Alwan, Faysal Galab, Mukhtar Bakri, and Shafel Mosed, all of Lackawana, New York, were arrested on charges of "providing, attempting to provide, and conspiring to provide material support and resources to designated terrorist organizations."[7] All six accused belonged to the Yemeni community of Lackawanna, just outside of Buffalo, and the news media dubbed them the "Lackawanna Six." The men were said to be members of the first homegrown jihadist group in the United States, and their case was approached with all the enthusiasm that could be expected from the law-enforcement officials of a nation that had just one year earlier suffered the pain of 9/11. At Mukhtar Bakri's interrogation, he admitted to having traveled with his colleagues to an al-Qaeda training camp in Afghanistan, where he had learned about jihad and how to fire weapons (Temple-Raston 2007, 8–9).

Unfortunately, for the group, their trial was in post-9/11 America. President Bush and Vice President Dick Cheney took personal interest in the case, which was conducted at the same time of the trial of the American Taliban, John Walker Lindh. This was the first major instance where the defendants were not prosecuted for a crime committed, but effectively for what they might have done. In fact, the prosecution never even offered evidence that the men ever planned to do anything. In the end, the six men received sentences ranging from seven to ten years.

Dina Temple-Raston, National Public Radio's FBI news correspondent in 2007, noted that in a study of more than 400 jihadists, the common bond was found to be alienation—a profile matched by the Lackawanna Six (Temple-Raston 2007, 113). Although American, they felt alienated from the society at large and they sought identity through group cohesiveness. They came together to form the "Arabian Knights" and discovered a new religiosity. They were told that corruption in the Muslim world was due to Western interference and immorality and that they had to retrieve this lost glory by assisting their oppressed coreligionists. They therefore traveled to Pakistan where they learned about weaponry and warfare. When they chose to rethink their stance, their association with al-Qaeda had already been established. Since this organization was labeled as an enemy outfit, the outcome of the case was never in doubt. While it is almost certain that these men would have been tried differently had 9/11 not occurred, the fact is that they did knowingly engage in collaboration with entities that had been deemed by the government of the United States as terrorist organizations. It was therefore unrealistic to assume that they would go unpunished if they were caught, or be acquitted simply by stating that they did not actually indulge in any overt operations against the United States.

While the case of the Lackawanna six raised questions about civil liberties, another accusation of Muslim involvement in planned terrorist activity was built on more solid evidence north of the American border, in Toronto, Canada. In June 2006, police in Toronto, Ontario arrested 18 people on several charges, among which were: planning to detonate truck bombs, to open fire in a crowded area, to storm the Canadian Broadcasting Center, the Canadian Parliament building, and the Canadian Security Intelligence Service (CSIS) headquarters, and to behead the Prime Minister, Stephen Harper.[8]

The case first came to light when two of the accused were stopped at the US–Canada border in 2006 while attempting to smuggle weapons into Canada. Police decided to monitor the conversations and communications of the two accused while they were in jail. The police recruited Mubin Shaikh, a member of the Toronto Muslim Community, to infiltrate a group to which these men belonged and to find out more about their activities. The court case reports indicate that the group of 18 were training and planning to take up a "global fight" and to procuring weapons for such activity.[9]

In a country such as Canada, long hailed for its absence of a gun culture, despite its proximity to the United States, details of the alleged plotting to commit terrorism were horrific in detail. After one training session in 2006, plans for an "Operation Badr" were discussed.[10] The idea was to storm Parliament Hill in the Canadian capital of Ottawa, take politicians hostage, and demand the removal of Canadian troops from Afghanistan. The group would also demand the release of all Muslim prisoners in Canada, and if their demands were not met, they would kill everyone.[11]

The perpetrators were sentenced to long terms in prison, but launched some rather interesting grounds of appeal. One ground was that of entrapment, alleging that the Canadian intelligence's agent, Mubin Shaikh, had in fact acted as an instigator to impressionable youths.[12] Although this appeal was dismissed, many Muslims have, on Facebook, taken Mubin Shaikh to task for seeking to put coreligionists in jail. The interaction on his Facebook page with coreligionists, supporters or opponents, is interesting as it provides a rather candid picture of the worldview of Muslim youth in North America, ranging from the liberal to the most harshly anti-Western bloc rhetoric. In many cases, the dominant rhetoric seems to be that Muslims are held to a different standard of culpability. This worldview does not seek to deny their involvement in subversive activity, but merely that the penalties are harsher for Muslim perpetrators.

On April 25, 2006, Hamid Hayat of Lodi, California was found guilty and sentenced to 24 four years in prison on the charge of lying to FBI agents and of having attended an al-Qaida training camp in Pakistan, to carry out acts of violence when returning to the United States. This was the state of California's first terrorism case dealing with travel to and training in foreign lands to commit violence in the United States. The sentence was appealed on the grounds that the jury foreperson was biased and that the Judge had allowed prejudicial evidence from witnesses for the prosecution while excluding testimony from defense witnesses.[13] On March 13, 2013, the appeal was turned down. It was ruled that Hamid Hayat had received a fair trial. The decision, however, was not unanimous. A. Wallace Tashima, one of the judges on the three-member 9th U.S. Circuit Court of Appeals, dissented, noting that "[t]he government asked a jury to deprive a man of his liberty largely based on dire, but vague, predictions that the defendant might commit unspecified crimes in the future."[14]

A new appeal, launched by attorney Dennis Riordan on July 6, 2014, argues several issues, among them that the interrogation was improperly conducted, that the then legal representative of Hayat was an inexperienced immigration lawyer, and that translations of documentation found on Hayat's person are actually more benign than those rendered by the Prosecution's witness.[15] As McGregor Scott, one of the state attorneys, noted, the expert's interpretation was "icing on the cake" for the prosecution's case (Waldman 2006, 90). It was also argued that other testimony the expert witness was allowed to give was beyond the limits of his specialty as he ventured into speculating about the state of mind of the accused, rather than restricting himself to the translation of the amulet. In the appeal, it would seem that some sort of attempt would have been made to focus on the use of the amulet as a regular charm worn by travelers. Regardless of how many "experts" were found to attest to this allegation, the fact remains that this is simply untrue. The Muslim tradition knows specific prayers for travelers, and the most well-known supplication can be heard in Arabic after the takeoff of any Saudi airline passenger plane: basically, it is asking that God make the journey bearable and ensure the safety of the travelers. The expert witness for the prosecution, a scholar trained in Saudi Arabia, noted that the translation of the amulet read, "Lord! Let us be at their throats, and we ask you to give us refuge from their evil" (Beauchamp 2010/11, 1108). Experts from within Pakistan at the time claimed that this supplication was not a well-known one. It seems, however, that from the time of the initial case to the present, the argument has been made that this is a popular incantation worn by travelers; however, the texts from which the prayer is derived, along with scholarly explanations, show it to be used by those who see themselves in enemy territory.

Is it possible that, as Justice A. Wallace Tashima has noted, this was a case of "anticipatory prosecution"? This is an issue that will be played out at the appeal hearings. For this research, however, the question regarding Hamid Hayat's innocence is important. Can it be argued that the testimony from witnesses who have now come forward to state that he did not attend training camp in any way evidences his innocence of any wrongdoing? Traveling to Pakistan and spending time in an al-Qaeda dominated region at the height of the terrorist scare are all things difficult to explain as evidence of victimization.

On May 27, 2009, suicide bombers attacked the Inter-Services Intelligence (ISI) headquarters in Lahore, Pakistan, injuring more than 300 people and killing approximately 30 others.[16] A propaganda video by al-Qaeda later revealed one of the bombers as Ali Jaleel, a Maldivian national, who became notorious as the first citizen from that country to be involved in suicide terrorism. Unknown to many followers of the news reports, the Maldivian authorities had long been on the trail of Ali Jaleel. In July of 2006, Maldivian authorities had arrested him, under suspicion of being a member of al-Qaeda. Under interrogation at Dhoonhido detention center in Male, he admitted to having pledged allegiance to Abu Isa Muhammad, who, in turn, had claimed the caliphate and leadership of Muslims and had recruited people to join his radical organization.[17] Cooperation between the Maldivian and American authorities resulted in uncovering an American supporter of Ali Jaleel. On May 5, 2013, the U.S. Attorney's office in Portland, Oregon, disclosed that it had arrested a naturalized American citizen on Pakistani origin, Reaz Qadir Khan, on charges of having provided material support to terrorists, knowing and intending that such support would be used to commit the crime of conspiring to kill, maim, or kidnap on foreign soil.

Initially, Mr. Khan's defense to the charges was that he had indeed provided financial assistance to Ali Jaleel in 2008 as well as to the latter's two wives in June of 2009. Such assistance, it was argued, did not in and of itself make Mr. Khan culpable of any crime unless he actually knew what Mr. Jaleel would do. Khan passed a polygraph test to show he had no knowledge of what Jaleel intended to perpetrate. At the government's expense, and to provide the proper rights of an accused under American law, expert witnesses were employed by the defense. It was also argued that conclusions reached by American intelligence and the State Attorney's office were based upon an improper understanding of Islamic law or of Pakistani culture. Faced, however, with the voluminous evidence of emails, interviews, wiretapped conversations, and coded messages between himself and Ali Jaleel, Khan suddenly pleaded guilty to providing advice and financial assistance to the individuals who carried out the suicide attack. His lawyers and the governmental attorney agreed on a sentence of 87 months[18] that was formally imposed on June 19, 2015.

Like many defendants in such cases, it is important to note that Mr. Khan's first line of defense was that he was simply doing an Islamic duty in helping those who were students and in dire need of financial help. A survey of the email exchange between Khan and Jaleel, however, revealed that both harbored negative perceptions of their coreligionists who did not share their radical ideas. For both of them, the true state of Islam could only be practiced if medieval interpretations of Shariah were in force, if a particular type of Arabic were spoken, and if Muslims were in absolute power. Though this can be seen as having a right to hold certain opinions, once the messages indicated that Jaleel knew he was on a suicide mission and that Khan had agreed to take care of his survivors, a guilty plea seemed the better route than a conviction: had he maintained his innocence, the maximum sentence could have been 15 years to life.

The matters covered thus far have involved the actions taken against Muslim defendants in criminal courts. The allegations of victimization have also been heard in civil courts, where accusations have been brought against state entities by Muslim citizens. One such case involved Sultaana Freeman, a former evangelist preacher, who had converted to Islam in 1997.[19] Her interpretation of Islam was one that required the covering of the face in the presence of strangers. Her allegation, as put forth by her attorney from the Association for Civil Liberties Union (ACLU), was that, according to Florida state law, the government should not substantially burden a person's exercise of religion. The attorney also went on to claim that fourteen states had exemptions for Christians whose interpretation of the second commandment to forbid graven images did not allow them to be photographed.[20] The plaintiff argued from several points, among them that picture identification documents are inherently flawed (since people can change their appearance) and that she was singled out simply because she is Muslim.[21]

On July 6, 2003, Judge Janet C. Thorpe ruled that Ms. Freeman's right to her exercise of religion would not be violated by having to show her face on her driver's license, noting that in the interests of security such photographs as a form of identification were essential.[22] The court also noted several inconsistencies between the plaintiff's claims and her actual practice. Ms. Freeman, while claiming that the photography of living beings was against her religious beliefs, had nonetheless agreed to be photographed while veiled; her husband, who had testified that the family held beliefs as a unit, had also allowed himself to be photographed for his driver's license.[23] The court also produced testimony to show that the state had tried as much as possible to allow for accommodations in similar instances. Finally, it was argued, that the plaintiff had not shown what substantial burden the state was imposing upon her in requesting to abide by the law. Law professor Robert Whorf noted that the state had in no way indicated that it was infringing upon the woman's right to her religious practice, but that it was a matter of security.[24]

Muslims weighed in on the matter too. Khalid Abou el-Fadl, professor of Islamic Law at UCLA, testified that the doctrine of necessity in Islamic law would allow for the woman to take a full-face photograph.[25] Here, Abou el-Fadl was referring to a condition adumbrated in the Islamic law maxim that states (in a functional translation): "necessity allows for allowability of that which would normally be forbidden" (*Al darura tajlib al taisir*). Other Muslims asserted that the case was frivolous and that the petitioner was in fact damaging the image of American Muslims.[26]

Conclusion

The scope of this study does not allow for coverage of numerous other cases of civil litigation on claims of religious discrimination against Muslims or of criminal convictions obtained against Muslims on charges related to terrorism. From the criminal cases covered in this study, however, it is clear that the perpetrators were involved in radical paths of Islam, at odds with scholarly and mainstream interpretations. Even in the case of Ms. Sultana Freeman, she admittedly was following the minority Salafi perspective, a perspective viewed as extremist even in conservative Saudi Arabia.[27] The role of such extremist interpretations must be considered before rushing to judgment about pervasive Islamophobia in the United States, Canada, or any of the Western bloc countries, given that the overwhelming majority of Muslims in those places seem to have little problem being productive citizens. The recent news coverage of the British Muslim "Jihadi John," who is allegedly the terrorist seen in Islamic State videos (known as ISIS, Islamic State in Syria and Iraq) beheading captives, suggests a man who felt that he was the victim of Islamophobia.[28] On March 18, 2015, for example, at Pine Bush High School, in upstate New York, students were allowed to recite the pledge of allegiance in various languages to commemorate National Foreign language week. The reading in Arabic was met with a storm of abuse by some students and activist groups, reaching a point where the school issued an apology for allowing such a reading in Arabic.[29] Groups such as al-Qaeda and the Islamic State thrive on such reports, trying to show Muslims and Arabs that Islamophobia goes beyond more than just a morbid hatred of Islam and that it extends to discrimination against those who speak Arabic, among whom are many non-Muslims. However, notwithstanding the prevalence of the admitted bigotries that afflict us, the sad fact remains—as it has been my intention to illustrate—that we still need to investigate every case carefully before subscribing to allegations of blanket Islamophobia.

Notes

1. Edward Said, 1980, "Islam through Western Eyes," *Nation*, August 26, http://www.thenation.com/article/islam-through-western-eyes (accessed February 18, 2015).
2. Sam Harris, 2010, "The Mosque," August 13, http://www.samharris.org/site/full_text/the-mosque (accessed February 4, 2015).
3. http://www.cbsnews.com/8301-503544_162-4943948-503544.html (accessed February 11, 2013).
4. http://www.cbspressexpress.com/cbs-news/releases/view?id=2199 (accessed February 11, 2013)
5. http://theamericanmuslim.org/tam.php/features/articles/rev.-franklin-graham (accessed February 11, 2013).
6. http://www.christianpost.com/news/franklin-grahamislam-is-not-faith-of-america-45041 (accessed February 11, 2013).
7. Khaleel Mohammed, 2007, "Six of a Kind," *San Diego Union Tribune* (Book Review Section), Sept. 16.
8. Isabel Teotonio, 2008, "Alleged Toronto Terror Plot Detailed in Court," *Toronto Star,* March 26.
9. Ibid.
10. Ibid.

11. Ibid.
12. Isabel Teotonio, 2009, "No Entrapment, court rules in terror case," *Toronto Star*, March 24.
13. "Hamid Hayat's Terror Conviction Upheld," *Lodi News*, March 13, 2013.
14. Ibid.
15. "Lodi Man's Terror Conviction Appealed, citing Defense Lapses," *San Francisco Chronicle*, May 2, 2014.
16. "Five Terrorists Arrested in Lahore," *Daily Nation*, Lahore, December 4, 2010.
17. Reference Folder RQK0000021, dated 06/01/2006, Expert Testimony Folder.
18. FBI press release, "Oregon Resident Pleads Guilty to Accessory after the fact in Connection with 2009 Suicide Bombing of ISI Headquarters in Pakistan," Portland, OR, February 13, 2015.
19. "Muslim Woman Sues State Over Driver's License," *Orlando Sentinel*, Jan 30, 2002, retrieved March 1, 2015, http://articles.orlandosentinel.com/2002-01-30/news/0201300347_1_state-of-florida-freeman-florida-license.
20. "Muslim Woman cannot wear veil in driver's license Photo," *USA Today*, June 6, 2003.
21. News.findlaw.com/cnn/docs/religion/frmnfl60603opn.pdf (accessed March 1, 2015).
22. "Muslim woman cannot wear veil in driver's license photo," *USA Today*, June 6, 2003.
23. News.findlaw.com/cnn/docs/religion/frmnfl60603opn.pdf (accessed March 1, 2015).
24. "Muslim Woman Sues State Over Driver's License," *Orlando Sentinel*, Jan 30, 2002, retrieved March 1, 2015, http://articles.orlandosentinel.com/2002-01-30/news/0201300347_1_state-of-florida-freeman-florida-license.
25. "Muslims don't see eye to eye," *Orlando Sentinel*, May 30, 2003.
26. Ibid.
27. News.findlaw.com/cnn/docs/religion/frmnfl60603opn.pdf (accessed March 1, 2015).
28. Ewan Palmer, 2015, "Jihadi John: Was 'gentle' Mohammed Emzawi radicalised due to harassment from UK security services?" *International Business Times*, February 26.
29. http://www.recordonline.com/article/20150318/NEWS/150319327 (accessed March 21, 2015).

Works Cited

Abdo, Genevieve, 2009, Mecca and Main Street: Muslim Life in America after 9/11, Oxford, NY: Oxford University Press.

Beauchamp, Peter, 2010/11, "Misinterpreted Justice: Problems with the Use of Islamic Legal Experts in U.S. Trial Courts," New York Law Review **55**, pp. 1098–119.

Cainkar, Louise, 2002, "No Longer Invisible: Arab and Muslim Exclusion after 9/11," Middle East Report **224** (Autumn), pp. 22–9.

Curtis IV, Edward, 2009, Muslims in America: A Short History, Oxford, NY: Oxford University Press.

Richardson, Robin, ed., 1997, Islamophobia: A Challenge for Us All, London: Runnymede Trust.

Said, Edward Said, 1997, Covering Islam, New York: Vintage Books.

Shaheen, Jack, 2003, "Reel Bad Arabs—How Hollywood Vilifies a People," Annals of the American Academy of Political and Social Science, vol. 588 Islam: Enduring Myths and Changing Realities, July, pp. 171–93.

Temple-Raston, Dina, 2007, The Jihad Next Door, New York: Perseus Books.

Waldman, Amy, 2006, "Prophetic Justice," Atlantic Monthly, October 1, pp. 82–93.

CROSSCURRENTS

THE NEXUS OF ENMITY
Ideology, Global Politics, and Identity in the Twenty-First Century

Eyal Bar

The twenty-first century, a little more than a decade in, appears to rival the twentieth century in the proliferation of struggles for recognition. It is characterized by the daily transgression of state boundaries by the global economy, by international law, by information and communication technologies, by disease, by clouds of radioactive air, and by corporeal bodies. In this era of globalization, the ability for states to affirm their separate existence and to maintain a boundary between what is inside and what is outside appears to be increasingly futile (Brown 2010). At the same time that state boundaries are exposed to these varied forms of penetration, we find states rapidly reorganizing in the face of pressure from civil society, opening space for the expression of new communal identities, whether in gay and gender rights, ethnic and minority rights, women's rights, immigrant rights, and to a lesser extent, the rights of the poor. Though this trend can be traced back to the early days of liberalism, it appears to have accelerated in the interwar and postwar years of the twentieth century as new nation-states emerged out of the crumbling colonial empires along ethno-religious lines. These nation-states operated on the principle that groups of peoples could best achieve peace if they were separated, given autonomy, and recognized as being equally entitled to so-called self-determination.

There are, however, two paradoxes that present themselves here. First, recognition for the purposes of self-determination relies on a discrete identity as the object of recognition while at the very same time it works to (re)construct identity. Second, the desire for recognition for the purpose of securing an identity opens the possibility of discrimination and insecurity on the basis of said identity. In this essay, I would like to address these paradoxes through the concept of separate-but-equal and the political ideologies that produce Islamophobia and anti-Semitism. In order to rid ourselves of these abusive ideologies, it might be necessary to conceive of group identity less as a stable end state that communities might achieve and more as a series of practices that require a flexible ethic of individual and group interrelations.

Traversing boundaries and identities

Much has been written on the ways in which modernization and global capitalism have implicated themselves in this process of nation-state formation, from Foucault's analysis of the shifting logic of power that emerged alongside the transition from feudal to mercantilist economy (Foucault 2004) to the accounts of national development proposed by Ernest Gellner (1983) and his contemporaries. For Gellner, Benedict Anderson (1983), Eric Hobsbawm (1990), and Michael Hechter (1973), among others, the institution of language, industrialization, and labor specialization (sometimes manifest as an ethnic/cultural division of labor) were crucial elements of nation-state formation. Local vernaculars, aided by advances in publication technologies and the growth of educational institutions, potentiated ethno-linguistic communities allowing for shared identity within a newly emerging social space. These same discursive forces that worked to define the boundaries of communities and bind their members together in a common identity have now revealed their ability to produce the reverse effect. As with global capital and the emerging global technological world (the world of Francis Fukuyama, Marshall McLuhan, or the National Security Agency), the networks that traverse national boundaries and link distant places into a community of common interests help to furrow the very channels that introduce once-alien elements into the very core of the body politic. The lines of flight reveal what Deleuze and Guattari (1987) identified as "Nomadology," a study of those forces that challenge the state-building project of boundary maintenance critical for statist and liberal capitalist projects.

It is within this context that the discourses of anti-Semitism and Islamophobia need to be understood. Both appear to enter our shared communal space after traveling across space and time: from the European landmass in the late nineteenth to early twentieth century, through the Middle East region in the post-WWII years, across the Atlantic and onto the shores of America and beyond in the twenty-first century. These discursive forces developed in large part through a series of events that many would desperately like to understand and describe in order to then manage and control them. The examples are many: in the Swiss legislation against a skyline punctured by minarets; in the dissemination of stage-crafted ISIS web-streams featuring brutal decapitations and immolations—with all the attendant props of an Islamic black flag and a soundtrack of Koran verses; in the kidnapping and murder of three Jewish youth from the Holy City; in the utter destruction and rising civilian death toll in "Hamastan," as Israel's Prime Minister likes to call the Gaza Strip; in the torture of anonymous Muslims in orange jumpsuits at black sites and at Guantanamo Bay; or in the murder of three young Muslims in North Carolina. In each case, the language and history we use to describe and explain these phenomena functions within a network of shared understandings that carry within them all manner of ideological and power-political positionings. In order to understand these ideological and political positions, an attempt to account for the historical processes guiding these worldviews appears critically important.

In the field of political science, rational choice theory often guides our understanding of political violence. In government institutions, the logic of security dictates all manner of invasive action against citizens and foreigners alike (e.g., NSA). Both logics suffer from an utter neglect of context. All too often, violent political events are dehistoricized, appearing as spontaneous psychoses of the body politic whose symptoms could be treated given the proper level of government and social intervention. The logics that emerge from rational choice theory and the security discourse depend upon both an abstraction and a normalization of social objects. As such, they work to cover-over histories and legacies that exert substantial influence on the subjectivities of the social objects they seek to manage. Our primary concern, I shall argue, should be centered on the legacies of colonialism and liberalism that continue to exert influence on our political projects. These are background conditions that too often evade our scrutiny despite their importance in framing our conventional understanding of political events.

The discourses that both promote and oppose Islamophobia and anti-Semitism potentially serve the projects of Western imperialism, neo-colonialism, and ethnocentrism when they are uncritically reproduced. They reveal a desperate attempt to demarcate the space between "us" and "them," to reproduce a Cartesian division of the social world that could guide our rational politics by simplifying our interactions along functionalist lines (Walker 1992). The threat of Islam (or the threat to secular society) in France is counteracted by *laïcité,* a policy that affirms a pure French national identity at the same time as it reveals (through a negative relation) the heterodox identity of the French citizenry that must be marginalized. In America, it is not uncommon to hear the demand placed on the Muslim community to monitor their members in order to allay the fears of violent manifestations of radical Islam on Main Street. It is taken for granted that an individual who might identify as Muslim is thereby held accountable for all other varied forms of Muslim identity. Similarly, the recent violence against Jewish communities in Europe appears to be guided by the presumptive complicity of all Jews for the violence perpetrated by the Israeli government. All these concerns have developed alongside the recent history of American and European military intervention and coercions in the "Muslim world." In Israel, the threat of an emerging fifth column, and the so-called demographic time bomb birthed from Palestinian wombs, is invoked while the occupation and colonialist roots of the state are actively marginalized in public and academic discourse. The U.S. war on terror continues under the guise of a security logic at the same time as it disavows, through silence, the violent legacy of Western hegemony over the Middle East.

I would like to explore the ideological compulsions that inform these discourses and work to buttress nation-building and state-building projects in the twenty-first century. This is not to discount the dangers of Islamophobia and anti-Semitism or weaken those projects aiming to limit their brutal manifestations, but rather to place these discourses in the context of power-political instrumentality. Situating these narratives in the countervailing and often contradictory forces of globalization and nationalism will help open a space for rethinking the ethic of recognition of group identity.

The nationalist state

Of the above works referenced, those that offer a teleological account of state formation risk calcifying and reifying community identity while at the same concealing this very process. In addition to cloaking the daily practices that work to re-affirm, alter, or reconstruct the nation-state, the narrative accounts of these thinkers tend to present the development of nationalism as guided by objective forces, without agency, almost as if nationalism were an expression of Hegelian *Geist* or an Aristotelian physics where objects move to their natural place. While the agency of elites is cited on occasion, the overall historiography is a positivist and teleological one. This view is best demonstrated by Gellner who explained that, "it is not the case that nationalism imposes homogeneity out of a willful cultural *Machtbedürfnis* [need for power]; it is the objective need for homogeneity which is reflected in nationalism" (Gellner 1983, 44). Nationalism as we know it developed in the only way possible, given the forces at play (i.e., industrialization), and lends itself to accounts that reaffirm the nation-state as the natural political category, whole onto itself, and relatively stable.

These works helped to contextualize nationalism within a particular historical epoch and greatly aided our ability to think about these political institutions in more sophisticated, abstract, and theoretical terms. However, in placing the process of nation-building in some distant past, we risk blinkering our view from the ongoing nation-state process, the active practice of state-building. Fortunately, there are places where we can cast our glance and see the ongoing nation-state process, not lost behind the dizzying momentum of cultural symbols, tradition, or taken-for-granted practices, but on the surface and openly acknowledged. Like astronomers scanning the skies to see the formation of nascent galaxies and extrapolate the birth of our own galaxy, we can cast our glance across the Atlantic toward the Middle East region. Doing so will help us understand the nation-state not as Genesis and origin, not as some product with a past, but rather as a political process which continues both abroad and in present-day America. This will also allow us to bring to the fore the relation of Western imperialism to the current discourse of Islamophobia and anti-Semitism.

Let us take as our first example the recent Jewish nationalism bill that was proposed by Benyamin Netanyahu's government in Israel. The bill sought to define Israel as the nation-state of the Jewish people and to inscribe this identity in law. The implications of this bill are varied and debatable, and I will not cover them in this short essay. For my present purposes, I would simply like to draw our attention to the reactions toward it. Almost immediately after the cabinet approved the proposal, the governing coalition disintegrated, precipitating a new round of elections held on March 17, 2015. The State proved itself incapable of securing agreement on a unified identity within its borders. This political event nicely demonstrates the background discourse of anti-Semitism and Islamophobia that drove efforts toward addressing localized symptoms of identity ambiguity. The ability to characterize the bill as an unproblematic action within the logic of self-determination depended upon a marginalization of the broader global political context. Could we think of the Jewish nationalism bill divorced from the dual history of Israeli colonialism and Palestinian violent resistance?

The bill, whether viewed as a defensive, securitizing strategy for Jewish hegemony over Israel or as an offensive strategy against the significant Palestinian minority in Israel (some 20 percent of the citizenry) can only be addressed in the broader historical context of a colonial project. This is not in itself a normative political position against Jewish colonialism, as the justice and justification of the Zionist project is a site of political contestation. It is only to say that placed out of context and invoked in tandem with the liberal ideals of self-determination, the event risks diverting our attention from the ways in which recognition can function as a violent imposition of a nationalist hegemony, as a modern variant of colonialism. Counter to the liberal notion of peaceful mutual recognition of separate identities, which comes uncomfortably close to the ideal of separate-but-equal, we need to consider the paradox of recognition as both liberation and confinement.

Turning to another example, we can set our gaze on the politics surrounding Daish (ISIS). Utilizing the nomad technology of the internet and video editing techniques to reproduce an esthetic that mimics Hollywood productions, Daish appears as a postmodern force *par excellence*. These forces are effectively rearranging the political space that was inherited from colonialism—in terms of control over the physical terrain, over the discursive field, and over the terrain of cyberspace—and co-opting the advent of the internet toward their neo-revanchist aims. British and American sympathizers have left the comforts of the liberal West to join the ranks of Daish. As recent news reports indicate, many of these volunteers are rather ignorant of the Islamic faith, some buying "Islam for Dummies" books, having not read or studied the Koran. And yet, the narrative that seems to dominate the mainstream is one of radical Islam (and by extension all of Islam) presenting a challenge to our Western liberal values.

This ideologically rich narrative is made manifest in the demand that Muslims the world over denounce the actions of ISIS, as if affinity is presumed until it is vocally renounced. Similarly, when the crows of the war on terror and Middle East intervention came home to roost, American Muslims were asked to undertake a special responsibility and monitor the activities of their compatriots. This demand, aside from standing on the flimsy empirical grounds that would demonstrate the great threat of radical Muslim violence in the U.S., diverts attention from the more general American political project which, for all intents and purposes, secures hegemony in the Middle East as if by right (Mitchell 2002). How might we theorize the politics concerning Daish without either emboldening Western hegemony over the Middle East or tolerating the ideology espoused by Daish and the practices undertaken by the group? How can Daish be denounced by Muslims without implying some natural national affiliation between these communities?

In each of these cases, the U.S. and Israeli governments appear as core sites that produce the dominant discourses and logics of these problematics. Both of their militaries are engaged in a series of conflicts that depend upon the radical othering of Islam and Arabs, already soft targets for prejudice. Both follow political projects that, in the name of modernity, democracy, and liberal values, seek to manage and estrange their respective Muslim/Arab subjects. Upon close scrutiny, these logics are parasitic on a cultural chauvinism that has its origins in colonial political projects (Said 1978).

New strategies toward ideology

If Russian President Vladmir Putin is accused of using nineteenth-century imperialism against Ukraine, then many of the states in our world can be accused of using twentieth-century nationalism against marginalized elements of their polities. In both cases, an impulsion toward demarcating and homogenizing social space is made apparent. Just as previous eras had to be overcome through the development of human reason and the elimination of human ignorance, so does ours need to overcome the prejudice borne of identity that continues to haunt the collective global social fabric. This would mean that instead of continuing the twentieth-century project of national self-determination, there needs to be a radical reassessment that focuses precisely on the project of nationalist and identity prejudice.

The discourses that framed nationalist movements, as soon as they proved useful tools for political power, became tools that could be wielded in a violent fashion under the guise of liberal equal rights. As the French case of *laïcité* demonstrates, the liberal urge for equal rights is already parasitic on an identity chauvinism that works to assimilate, homogenize, and manage various life worlds. In the name of freedom, these approaches advance constraints on the possible social and political imaginings that we might conjure. Through these ideologies of identity, the demand that Muslims renounce Daish can appear seemingly reasonable. Similarly, the blame cast on Jews the world over for the policies of the Israeli government are strengthened by the presumptive affiliation between Judaism and nationalism. In either case, the identity politics appears necessary for modern-day nationalism to function within an era of so-called globalization. Without recourse to identity, the imperative to manage and maintain power-political hierarchies through the division of the sociopolitical terrain (i.e., nationalism) would be rendered impotent. The first step toward eliminating the recent forms of prejudicial political violence is the recognition that modern identity politics militates against a world where physical barriers, political boundaries, and discursive networks are rapidly reorganizing.

How would Jewish and Islamic nationalism appear to us if they were robbed of their primary coercive mechanism—namely the compulsory proclamation of a sociocultural identity? They would appear as discourses and philosophies on living. They would appear as a series of propositions as to the good life that every individual should wish to achieve. They would then be a set of discourses that every individual could utilize and consider without any necessary contradiction to their (now expelled) identity. They would open radically new forms of thinking-being-in-the-world. They would, in short, turn into political philosophies rather than power-political ideologies.

This must strike some readers as idealistic-though-misguided at best and dangerously naïve at worst. Yet, upon an empirical investigation of the current world and world history, it seems that the burden of proof for the liberal identity politics should be placed on those who speak in its name. After all, in no historical era has the concept of separate-but-equal bore the fruit of peaceable society and pacific relations—at least not without a whole arsenal of coercions and threats that lurk in the background.

By appreciating the paradox of recognition, we can begin to address the violent implications of identity politics and avoid political projects that privilege stability at the expense of fluidity. We should hesitate to enact barriers in a world otherwise marked by rapid changes in social and political space.

Works Cited

Anderson, Benedict, 1983, Imagined Communities: Reflections on the Origin and Spread of Nationalism, London: Verso.

Brown, Wendy, 2010, Walled States, Waning Sovereignty, New York: Zone Books.

Deleuze, Gilles, and Felix Guattari, 1987, A Thousand Plateaus: Capitalism and Schizophrenia, trans. Brian Massumi, Minneapolis: University of Minnesota Press.

Foucault, Michel, 2004, Security, Territory, Population, trans. Graham Burchell, New York: Picador.

Gellner, Ernest, 1983, Nations and Nationalism, Ithaca: Cornell University Press.

Hechter, Michael, 1973, Internal Colonialism: The Celtic Fringe in British National Development, New Brunswick: Transaction Publishers.

Hobsbawm, E.J., 1990, Nations and Nationalism since 1780: Program, Myth, Reality, Cambridge: Cambridge University Press.

Mitchell, Timothy, 2002, "McJihad: Islam in the U.S. Global Order," Social Text **20/4** (Winter), pp. 1–18.

Said, Edward W., 1978, Orientalism: Western Conceptions of the Orient, New York: Penguin Books.

Walker, R.B.J., 1992, Inside/Outside: International Relations as Political Theory, Cambridge: Cambridge University Press.

CONTRIBUTORS

Melanie Adrian holds a PhD in Social Anthropology and the Study of Religion from Harvard University. She is currently on faculty in the Department of Law and Legal Studies at Carleton University, Ottawa, Canada. Her research focuses on the question of rights of minorities in religiously, ethnically, and culturally diverse societies. Her book, *Religious Freedom at Risk: The EU, French schools, and Why the Veil was Banned*, will be out in the fall of 2015.

Mehnaz M. Afridi is Assistant Professor of Religious Studies and Director of Holocaust, Genocide, and Interfaith Education Center at Manhattan College, Riverdale, NY. She is committed to interfaith work, contemporary Islam, and Holocaust education. She teaches a variety of courses on Islam, world religions, genocide studies, and contemporary Islamic literature. Her articles include "The Role of Muslims and the Holocaust" in *Oxford Handbooks Online* (2014). She is coeditor of *Orhan Pamuk and Global Literature: Existentialism and Politics* (2012) and is working on her forthcoming book, *Shoah through Muslim Eyes* (2016).

Alex Alvarez, PhD, is Professor in the Department of Criminology and Criminal Justice at Northern Arizona University and was the founding Director of the Martin-Springer Institute for Teaching the Holocaust, Tolerance, and Humanitarian Values. His main areas of study are in collective and interpersonal violence. His books include the following: *Governments, Citizens, and Genocide* (2001); *Murder American Style* (2002); *Violence: the Enduring Problem* (2013); *Genocidal Crimes* (2009); and *Native America and the Question of Genocide* (2014). He has also served as an editor for the journal *Violence and Victims*, was a founding coeditor of the journal *Genocide Studies and Prevention*, was a coeditor of the H-Genocide List Serve, and is an editorial board member for a number of journals. He has been invited to speak and present his research in various countries such as Austria, Bosnia, Canada, England, Germany, the Netherlands, Lithuania, and Sweden.

Eyal Bar is a PhD Candidate in the School of Politics and Global Studies at Arizona State University. His research interests include the concept of recognition, the Israel–Palestine conflict, U.S. Foreign Policy, Critical International Relations Theory, Continental Philosophy, The History of the Political Science Field, and Enmity. He earned his MA in Middle East Studies from Ben-Gurion University of the Negev in Be'er Sheva for his dissertation entitled "Sovereignty in Crisis: A Case Study of Post-Disengagement Gaza." He has taught courses on the Israel–Palestine conflict and on Global Politics. Expecting to receive his PhD in spring 2016, he wishes to pursue a career as an educator and researcher at an institution of higher education.

Michael Dobkowski received his MA and PhD degrees in history from New York University and is presently Professor of Religious Studies at Hobart and William Smith Colleges and chair of the department. He is the author of *The Tarnished Dream: The basis of American Anti-Semitism* (1979), *The Politics of Indifference: Documentary History of Holocaust Victims in America* (1982), and *Jewish American Voluntary Organizations* (1986), and he coauthored *Nuclear Weapons, Nuclear States and Terrorism* (2007). He has cowritten and edited other volumes on the Holocaust, genocide, nuclear weapons, and anti-Semitism including the following: *The Nuclear Predicament: Nuclear Weapons in the 21st Century* (2000); and *On the Edge of Scarcity* (2003). His main areas of interest include the American Jewish experience, Holocaust Studies, religion and violence, terrorism, and anti-Semitism.

David Kader teaches in the areas of criminal procedure, torts, state constitutional law, and religion and the Constitution. Before joining the faculty at Arizona State University in 1979, he taught at Warwick University, England, and the University of Iowa. He served as Associate Dean of the law school at ASU from 1980 to 1983. He has been Visiting Professor of Law at various U.S. universities as well as Southampton University (England), Wuhan University (China), and Sarajevo University (Bosnia–Herzegovina). He also taught in the Arizona Center of Medieval and Renaissance Studies Summer Abroad Program at Cambridge University, participated in a NEH Summer Seminar at the Oxford Center for Hebrew and Jewish Studies, and was Visiting Fellow at the University of London Institute for Advanced Legal Studies. His work has taken him to the Balkans and to Turkey as part of an Arizona delegation under the auspices of the Foundation for Inter-Cultural Dialogue. Among his recent publications is the coedited *Poetry of the Law: From Chaucer to the Present* (2010).

Ethan Katz received his PhD from the University of Wisconsin and, since 2010, has been an Assistant Professor of History and Affiliated Professor of Judaic Studies at the University of Cincinnati. His book *The Burdens of Brotherhood* will be published by Harvard University Press in the fall of 2015. He is also the coeditor of *Secularism in Question: Jews and Judaism in Modern Times* (2015). Katz's work has been supported by a *Bourse Chateaubriand* from the French Foreign Ministry and by fellowships from, among others, the Society for French Historical Studies, the Center for Advanced Judaic Studies at the University of Pennsylvania, and the Foundation for Jewish Culture. He has previously published articles in English and French in journals, including *Jewish Quarterly Review*, *Journal of North African Studies*, *Diasporas*, and *Histoire et Société*, as well as for more popular audiences in the *Marginalia Review of Books* and *The Cincinnati Enquirer*.

C. Richard King is Professor of Critical Culture, Gender, and Race Studies at Washington State University. He has written extensively on Native American mascots, the changing contours of race in post–Civil Rights America, and the colonial legacies and postcolonial predicaments of American culture. Much of his current work focuses on white power movements and ideologies. He is the author/editor of several books, including the following: *Team Spirits: The Native American Mascot Controversy* (2001); *Postcolonial America* (2000); and *Unsettling America: The Uses of Indianness in the 21st Century* (2013). He has recently completed *Beyond Hate: White Power and Popular Culture* (2014).

Björn Krondorfer, PhD, is Director of the Martin-Springer Institute at Northern Arizona University and Endowed Professor of Religious Studies in the Department of Comparative Cultural Studies. His field of expertise is religion, gender, culture, (post-) Holocaust studies, Western religious thought, and reconciliation studies. He is the recipient of the Norton Dodge Award for Scholarly and Creative Achievements. He authored and edited ten books, among them *Male Confessions: Intimate Revelations and the Religious Imagination* (2010), *Men and Masculinities in Christianity and Judaism* (2009), and *Remembrance and Reconciliation* (1995) as well as three volumes in German on the cultural and theological legacy of the Holocaust. He guest-edited two journal issues ("Masculinities and Religion: Continuities and Change," *Religion and Gender* 2012, and "Embattled Masculinities in the Religious Traditions," *CrossCurrents* 2011). His scholarship helped to define the field of Critical Men's Studies in Religion. Currently, he explores connections between memory, trauma, and social/moral repair. He has been invited to speak, present his research, and facilitate intercultural encounters in Germany, South Africa, Australia, South Korea, Finland, Poland, United Kingdom, Italy, Israel/Palestine, Switzerland, Austria, and Canada.

Mohamed Mosaad Abdelaziz Mohamed is Assistant Professor of Sociology at the Department of Sociology and Social Work, Northern Arizona University. He received a PhD in religious studies from Emory University, and a master in anthropology and sociology from the American University in Cairo. Before that, Mohamed, a medical doctor, had worked as an orthopedist and psychiatrist. He focuses in his teaching and research on sociology of religion, modern Islam, political Islam, sociolinguistics, discourse analysis, modern and contemporary social theory, and sociology of globalization. His publications include the chapters "The New Trend of the Muslim Brotherhood in Egypt" (in *Whatever Happened to the Islamists?*, 2012) and "Ibn 'Aṭā' Allāh: A 'Ālim, Faqīh and Ṣūfī" (in *Sufism, Pluralism and Democracy*, 2015). He has been active for two decades in peace movements and interfaith dialogue groups.

CONTRIBUTORS

Khaleel Mohammed is professor and undergraduate adviser in the Department of Religious Studies at San Diego State University. After having studied Islamic Law in Saudi Arabia, he completed his graduate studies at Concordia and McGill Universities in Montreal, Canada. He also completed a Kraft-Hiatt postdoctoral fellowship at Brandeis University. He has authored several journal articles in shared narratives between the Abrahamic religions, interfaith relations, and Islamic law and has served as an expert witness in several terrorism cases in the United States.

www.ingramcontent.com/pod-product-compliance
Lightning Source LLC
Chambersburg PA
CBHW040300170426
43193CB00020B/2956